Britain's Last Battleships

Second edition

Britain's Last Battleships

Second edition

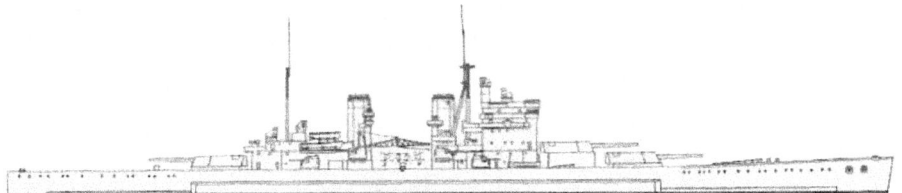

MATTHEW WRIGHT

This book is copyright and subject to international treaties. No part may be copied, reproduced, or otherwise duplicated by any means, without prior permission of the copyright holder.

Copyright © Matthew Wright 2018 and 2020

The moral rights of the author have been asserted.

Design copyright © Intruder Books 2020
Cover art copyright © Matthew Wright 2018
Drawing of HMS *Lion* (1938) by 'Admiral Killer', used in chapter headers under CC by-SA 4.0 license.

First published by Intruder Books, Wellington, 2018
This edition published by Intruder Books, Wellington, 2020.

ISBN 978-0-908318-28-5 (Intruder Books)

This book is part of the Intruder Books Monograph Series. Collect the set.

www.matthewwright.net
www.mjwrightnz.wordpress.com
www.facebook.com/MatthewWrightNZ

Contents

Introduction		1
1	Economic stagnation	3
2	Industrial constraints	13
3	The lure of second hand guns	24
4	War limitations	35
Notes		42
Bibliography		52

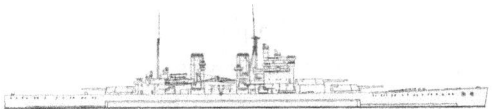

Introduction

The purpose of this short book – a monograph – is to trace the way British naval designers of the 1930s and early 1940s were bouncing against a mix of economic, treaty, engineering and financial limitations which were shared by few other nations; yet still sought to build the very best capital ships they could, to meet national need in terms of government strategic vision, and the tactical approaches the Admiralty took to sea battles at the time. As such this extended essay is not intended to be a 'complete' description or data-listing of Britain's battleships of the day; it is written to purpose, exploring the people and context of an era.

The focus is on the framework around the last generation of Britain's battleships; the political, economic, industrial and practical limits that shaped the decisions made by Britain's naval designers. These included not just the diplomacy of the inter-war Treaty system, but the decline of British industry, significant limits to Britain's support infrastructure, notably docks, and the strictures of war at a time when the whole of Britain's war effort suffered similar limitations.

The resulting ships have often been criticised for their apparent lack of gun-power and various design flaws which, allegedly, made them the least of all the new-generation battleships of the Second World War. Britain's most powerful battleship class of this generation, the Lions, were overtaken by war and never completed; and the only other battleship the British finished was HMS *Vanguard*, completed after war's end and fitted with second-hand

15-inch guns left over from the First World War.

All the decisions that led to these characteristics, however, fall into place when set against the wider context. And there was one other factor that also has to be considered. Britain's empire was fading; but it was difficult for many in it to accept the point. British Admiralty, in particular, remained largely fixed in a mind-set of past generations. Britain had once ruled the waves; and the realities of the decline in that Empire were intellectually accepted – but the spiritual and emotional mind-set was still, ultimately, that of Britain in the high noontide of its power, forty or fifty years earlier. The result had due effect on Britain's last battleships.

Matthew Wright
March 2020

CHAPTER ONE

Economic stagnation

On 4 August 1960, the Royal Navy's last battleship, HMS *Vanguard*, was towed from her berth in Portsmouth harbour for her final voyage: a journey to the breakers at Faslane. Her immediate predecessors, the four surviving battleships of the *King George V* class, had already gone to the scrapyard in the late 1950s. None were particularly old, as battleships go – and all were well below the average age of the battleships with which Britain had entered the Second World War in 1939. Youth did not save them. In the new age of supersonic jet bombers, nuclear weapons, guided missiles and incipient space-flight, battleships seemed an anachronism, a hang-over from an age when warfare was, somehow, more romantic. They still had uses – notably for shore bombardment – but only the richest navies could justify the expense of keeping large ships in service for such limited function. And by 1960, the Royal Navy had long since lost that sort of funding.

Vanguard did not go without a fight. At 10.35 am she ran aground at Portsmouth Point and was only stopped from ramming the *Still and West* public house by her pilot, R. D. Ottley, who ordered the anchor dropped at the right moment to catch chains slung across the harbour to guide an old car ferry. The the tide was ebbing; there was a risk she might swing across to Fort Blockhouse, potentially becoming a wreck and obstructing access to the main harbour until she could be cleared.[1] Fortunately help was to hand.

The ocean-going tugs that had been intended to take up the tow outside harbour were brought in, and with their power the battleship was dragged free after about three-quarters of an hour.

So ended an era in British naval history that, by one vision, had begun a century earlier when Britain's first two iron-built, steam-driven frigates, *Warrior* and *Black Prince*, took to the water – ships that were, effectively, the battleships of their age, as powerful as the heaviest ships the French of the day could muster.[2] Or we might assign the beginning of Britain's late industrial-era battleship age instead, to 1869 when HMS *Devastation* – Britain's first mastless turret battleship – was laid down.[3] By another measure, perhaps the story behind Britain's last ever battleship might have begun in 1905-06 when HMS *Dreadnought*, Britain's first all-big-gun battleship – and a direct conceptual ancestor of *Vanguard* by virtue of turbine propulsion and an all-big-gun armament – was built.[4] The specifics are academic; industrial technology insinuated itself into nineteenth century naval construction by degrees and by evolution, making it difficult to pin down a particular ship or year as a start-point for Britain's era of industrial-technology battleships.

The end, however, was more sharply defined; and it came not on the back of a further technological revolution, but because of ongoing penury and industrial decline – a decline that the Second World War underscored. Post-Second World War Britain did not have the money or resources to maintain battleships, however much they were wanted by sections of the Admiralty. But this decline had not emerged out of a vacuum. And that is the point of this book. Britain had been declining financially and industrially since the end of the First World War, and the constraints shaped the generation of British battleships that emerged during the 1930s, of which *Vanguard* was the end product. Even the international naval treaty system that limited the broad parameters of these ships was largely a British innovation by the 1930s, driven by a Treasury imperative to cut costs. The infrastructure limits that also dogged Britain's 1930s-era battleship generation – notably through the scale of docking facility – were another consequence of this wider economic position.

To understand the issues, we first have to explore the context of Britain's industrial and financial position during the inter-war years. This was far from prosperous. The First World War had levied an enormous cost on Britain and its Empire, first and foremost in lives – meaning that the 1920s were tinged with social-scale grief as a population mourned the 'lost generation'.

There was also a heavy financial cost. By 1918, war expenditure had risen to 47 percent of Britain's gross domestic product, the usual measure of national wealth.

This was an enormous sum to pour into a single purpose – particularly because resources diverted to fighting, notably manpower, had to be taken off the labour force and offered no wider productive return to the economy. Some of the war expenditure did cycle back into the economy, notably through wages. But much of it was simply lost because the munitions and material it produced were destroyed. The war, in short, did not merely come with a horrific cost in life; it also, quite literally, burned money and expended, without return to the economy, the productive labour that went into making the *materiel*. And the First World War was fought to an astonishing scale. The enormous cost to Britain of supporting their war effort was paid for in part by debt, in part by simply printing money; Britain went off the gold standard and instead established the pound on a fiat (legal) basis.[5]

Of course such a huge diversion of national wealth into warfare could not be long sustained, and afterwards the problem became paying for it. Part of the cost of the war was eventually levied against Germany via war reparations. In essence, the inflationary effect of printing money was exported to them instead. However, that did not avert all of Britain's problems. By 1919 the national debt stood at 135 percent of GDP, rising to 181 percent in 1923. This was a huge amount to have to pay back, not helped by the fact that interest payments alone stood at around 7 percent of GDP.[6] Things might have been easier if the economy was booming; but it was not. A brief post-war boom in 1919-20 swiftly gave way to a sharp recession in which unemployment rose to about ten percent – and stayed there for much of the inter-war period. The British economy was stagnant: real growth in the gross domestic product – that is, the growth of GDP corrected for inflation – was close to zero.

The official government answer was to slash spending, notably on matters military. The fact that this took money out of the economy was observed by such economists as John Maynard Keynes, who eventually came up with other approaches.[7] But that did not stop a policy of constraint being applied for much of the inter-war period. In August 1919 the Secretary of State for War and Air, Winston Churchill, proposed a 'ten year rule', by which the services were instructed to plan on not having to fight another war for ten years. Although new political oppositions were already evident at the time, notably in regard to the Soviet Union, with whom Britain was technically at war in 1918-19 via the Allied intervention against the Bolsheviks – to suppose no major war for a decade was reasonable in the wake of the 'war to end all wars'. The primary enemy had been defeated. Defence spending fell to less than pre-war levels, and was below three percent of GDP by the early 1920s. For the Royal Navy – and for Britain's armed services in general – these were hard times, which Winston Churchill later dubbed the 'locust years'.[8]

Britain's main defence problem was that her empire carried world-spanning obligations for the navy. It was changing in nature; Britain was deliberately devolving power to the larger colonies – Canada, Australia, Britain, New Zealand and South Africa particularly, which had become self-governing Dominions. That constitutional shift continued during the 1930s. But Britain still had other colonies, worldwide; and demand for trade protection did not go away. Indeed, keeping the sea lanes open became increasingly crucial as Britain sought to resolve its economic issues by trading with its own Empire, and as oppositions began to grow with Japan, throwing focus on Far Eastern defence.

The more immediate issue in 1919-20 was that Britain's post-war economic bubble burst just as a new naval race was brewing between Japan and the United States, pivoting around battleships and battlecruisers of exceptional size, speed and fire-power.[9] Britain's naval problem in 1919 was threefold. First, although they ended the war with immense numeric superiority, their 12-inch gunned capital ships were obsolescent and even the 13.5- and 15-inch gunned ships were not up to the scale of the new Japanese and US monsters.[10] Second, the government was looking at major military cut-backs. in July 1919 the Chancellor of the Exchequer, Austin Chamberlain, urged Cabinet to slash the Royal Navy to 15 capital ships in commission, with more cuts in 1920.[11]

The third and perhaps more subtle issue was that ship design had undergone a dramatic revolution during the First World War, in part because armour-piercing shells had been re-designed to become more effective after the battle of Jutland, in part because battle experience offered useful engineering and procedural lessons. Better shells demanded better armour to protect the ship's vitals, an evolutionary shift in which even battleships were now regarded as potentially vulnerable if they were not better armoured, an issue reflecting not just thickness but also distribution of that protection.

The problem was that no British ship met the very latest thinking - not even HMS *Hood*, the first of four planned 'Admiral' class battlecruisers.[12] Thanks to a complex design evolution that reflected fast-changing British thinking about protection, she was better armoured than any First World War battleship.[13] But even this was not thought sufficient. In 1919, live-fire tests of new-type 15-inch shells against a structure representing the armour protection of *Hood*, underscored doubts about the design.[14]

That year the Admiralty began considering its post-war plans, which had to take new Japanese construction, particularly, into account. The decision was taken to finish *Hood* – which was well advanced – cancel the other three 'Admirals', and develop new heavy ships to the latest concepts. Serious design work began on a new generation of heavy ships, of scale to match the new US and Japanese ships – which implied 16 or 18 inch guns – and incorporating the latest thinking in regard to armour protection, among other war lessons. A variety of battlecruiser designs were considered, given alphabetic tags – backwards, starting from K, to differentiate them from a series of battleship designs. These began at L and moved the other way through the alphabet.[15]

Britain's new post-war construction programme, developed apparently by the First Sea Lord, Admiral Sir David Beatty, eventually revolved around four battlecruisers, expected to be ordered in 1921; and four battleships projected for order in 1922.[16] Industry could certainly support this proposed schedule which, in effect, returned construction to the pace of pre-war years when the Royal Navy had typically been able to order four capital ships annually. Indeed, the scale of Britain's pre-war ship-building industry had been such that it could support not only these orders, but simultaneously build similarly-sized ships for foreign powers.[17] Indeed, there were arguments that such a programme was necessary to keep the industry alive.

These were not the only factors confronting the Admiralty at the turn of the 1920s. Any new ships were going to have to be of unprecedented scale to match the Japanese and US monsters; but available docking facilities limited both dimensions and displacement. The likely maximum was thought to be around 48,000 tons – a limit swiftly reached for the battlecruisers because of the need to shoe-horn up to nine 16-inch guns and propulsion for 32 knots into a hull, along with the scale of armour now thought necessary. That demanded efficiencies, which were found from two innovations. The first was to mount the sloped side armour belt internally. This meant it could be sloped further, improving resistance against incoming shells and reducing the thickness and weight. The second was to apply a unique arrangement of triple turrets, clustered around a new-style superstructure. The turret arrangement meant that the heavy armour now demanded for magazine protection could be concentrated into a short space, saving weight. The down-side was that the third 16-inch turret, placed amidships, could not fire directly aft; but that was accepted, in part on the basis of war experience.[18]

War experience also entered the mix, not least in new 'tower' bridge superstructure which – by contrast with earlier designs – was not merely monolithic, but also lacked a heavy conning tower. This was a consequence of war experience in which officers, repeatedly, had stood outside to see what was going on; and where there had been a premium on superstructure space to support ship command functions and increasing array of fire-control and other apparatus. The criticism of 'tower' bridges – that they created a larger target and did not really protect the men – was valid, but the benefits were thought to out-weigh the down-side.

None of this was cheap: the estimated price per ship was some £9 million, enough to buy three *Royal Sovereign* class battleships.[19] This underscored the fact that the real cost – in economic terms, the cost corrected for inflation - of defence equipment always rose, driven in this case partly by increased scale but also by the fact that the ships were becoming more complex, and the cost of what went into them was rising in an absolute sense. To give that trend due perspective, once the effects of inflation are calculated, £9 million in 1921 values was the equivalent in 2018 money of £382.5 million,[20] a significant figure but still well below the approximate £1.05 thousand million unit cost of Britain's largest non-aviation surface combatants of the 2010s, their Type 45 destroyers.[21]

Actually getting the ships, however, was another matter. The Prime Minister, David Lloyd-George, was opposed to a capital ship programme, and in December 1920 forbad the Admiralty to build further capital ships until wartime lessons and the 'place and usefulness of the capital ship in future naval operations' had been investigated.[22] That put the Admiralty into direct conflict with a Committee of Imperial Defence sub-committee conducting the investigation. The First Sea Lord, Admiral Sir David Beatty, refused to back down, was supported by Winston Churchill; and the upshot was a further political fracas.[23]

However, while some Committee members were in favour of more capital ships, no firm conclusions were reached; but the new 'one-power' standard remained alive. During the first two weeks of March 1921, Lloyd-George decided to allow the Admiralty to include starting funds for four of the eight capital ships they wanted; but only the first £15 million of the £75 million cost of the whole multi-year programme.[24] The draft naval estimates for 1921-22 were approved on 17 March with provision to start the four battlecruisers. However, when the Admiralty approached the Chancellor of the Exchequer, Austen Chamberlain, for approval to order long-lead items – guns and armour – they were refused. Cabinet had not confirmed the spending. Nor did Lloyd-George's government now consider the matter.[25] By this time the United States was making noises about an arms limitation treaty, and Cabinet anticipated one. That took any priority out of acceding to Admiralty requests.[26] However, at the Imperial Conference held in June 1921, the Admiralty persuaded Britain's self-governing Dominions to provide 2.2 million pounds towards the new ships, siphoned from their share of German war reparations.[27] Armed with that promise, Beatty approached Cabinet on 21 July.

This time he met a more favourable reception, in part because the original March arrangement had been on the basis of the Dominions providing something – but more particularly because by this time President Harding had invited participation in an international disarmament conference to be held in Washington that November. The British, whose fleet was largely obsolescent - needed a bargaining counter. The new battlecruisers were it.[28]

Orders for the new battlecruisers – Design G3, the last of a series of iterations - were placed in August 1921. They were never assigned formal names.[29] Work began on the guns and mountings, and metal was apparently cut by Swan Hunter. Design work was also under way on the 1922 battleship class, but the whole programme was suspended while Britain attended a conference to discuss naval arms limitation in Washington.[30]

The 'Washington Treaty' of early 1922 – formally, the 'Five Power Treaty'[31] – scrapped virtually all the new-build ships by Japan, Britain and the United States, slashed fleet sizes to defined levels, imposed a 'battleship holiday' of ten years, set a maximum lifespan for existing ships, and restricted replacements to 35,000 tons and 16-inch guns. In compensation for the fact that Japan and the United States had already completed new 16-inch gunned ships, Britain was allowed to build two new battleships, but only to Treaty limits. That cut out any chance of two G3's being completed, although the Admiralty argued the point. The ships that followed - the *Nelsons* - used the 16-inch guns and mountings ordered for the first two G3's, and were designed to the new displacement limit; but were otherwise the next iteration of the 1921-22 battleship design series.[32]

The point about this treaty is that it played into the British requirement to keep costs down. That became a priority during the 1920s when the Treasury pushed the Admiralty to consider smaller battleship designs for cost reasons. Those strictures fed into the Geneva Naval Conference of 1927, called by US President Calvin Coolidge between the signatories of the Five Power Treaty to discuss further arms limitations. For Britain the issue was balancing cost-cutting with the need to have enough ships to patrol their far-flung Empire and protect trade. This stood against US proposals, and the conference broke up without agreement.[33] However, cost constraints remained and the 'ten year rule' was made permanent in 1928, automatically rolling over each year.

The same international political issues emerged at the London Naval Conference of early 1930, where the British were again looking for ship numbers and cost reductions. However, because of the sharp economic downturn of the day – part of the slide into the Great Depression that struck the west during 1930-31 – US delegates were in more receptive mood. The outcome was a treaty that, among other things, extended the original 'battleship holiday' by five years to 1936.[34]

By the early 1930s, however, it was clear the world was becoming a more dangerous place. The rise of totalitarian fascism in the central powers, Germany and Italy, was matched by totalitarian communism in the Soviet Union, under Joseph Stalin. And Britain's Far East possessions were threatened by a militarist Japanese. The naval treaty system was under strain, and although the British hoped it would continue, for financial reasons, the political reality by 1935 – as work began on a new treaty – was that it probably would not.

In 1933 Britain's Director of Naval Construction, Sir Arthur Johns, began working on the Royal Navy's first battleships since the *Nelson* class.[35] The 'battleship holiday' promised by the Five Power Treaty of 1922 and the London Naval Treaty of 1930 was due to expire in 1936. While it was theoretically renewable, the chances seemed to be reducing with every new international crisis. By the mid-1930s the world's three remaining global-power scale democracies – Britain, France and the United States – were not merely beset with economic recession but also seemed to be on the back foot against a rising tide of violence and totalitarianism. Japan was already at war with China, which infringed on European interests. The Soviet Union had become a totalitarian dictatorship built around economic ideas that were opposed to those of the west and built on an ideology that pivoted on the downfall of capitalism. Italian ambitions in North Africa were provoking concerns; and in Germany, the Nazi party had been actually elected, despite a standing repute for being extremists. While the western democracies – Britain, the United States and France – hoped for the best, there was every potential that the world might plunge into ongoing crisis and war. From the British and French perspective, the fact that the United States also had a relatively isolationist foreign policy simply increased the concern.

From the naval perspective Britain – like the other major powers – had to consider what might be built as the treaty system staggered under these international pressures. Johns' team in the Department of Naval Construction included Stanley Goodall – who became DNC in 1936 – and the battleship specialist, Herbert S. Pengelly. The limitations the Admiralty faced were manifold. The specifics were limited not just by treaty, but also by a lack of skilled naval draftsmen and reduced industrial capacity.[36] Britain's arms industry, particularly, was run. A cluster of closures, amalgamations and a quick-fire shedding of peripheral interests by the major firms, peaking in 1927-28, re-shaped the field on a significantly smaller scale.[37]

The fundamental limit was financial. The 1920s did not 'roar' for Britain; the country and, to some extent, her Empire and Commonwealth, missed out on the post-war boom that swept the United States. One of the specific outcomes of the general decline in defence spending and the dramatic reductions of British industrial and steel output was a commensurate reduction in the ability to build heavy warships, and in particular their gun mountings.[38] Steel production, for instance, stayed below 10,000,000 tons for much of the period, and at times was as low as 4,000,000.[39] Former major ship-building and defence firms were forced to either close or amalgamate; and the consolidations of the 1920s, particularly, were crippling for a naval construction industry that, pre-First World War, had been the largest in the world. Britain's battleship programme had to take its place alongside a rearmament programme that included new classes of aircraft carrier, destroyers, cruisers and submarines.

One outcome was that the Great Depression of the early 1930s hit

Britain very hard. Industrial output fell by a third between 1929 and 1933, trade dropped by half, and by 1932 some 3.5 million were unemployed – notably in the industrial regions where the unemployment rate was as high as 70 percent.[40] While economists such as John Maynard Keynes had new approaches to resolve the problems, the main government response was conservative. An emergency budget in September 1931 slashed public spending, including public sector wages. This provoked, among other things, active opposition in the Royal Navy where sailors in the Atlantic Fleet staged a mutiny to protest the pay cuts on 14-15 September, in turn provoking a brief stock-market panic and causing the government to again abandon the gold standard a week later.[41]

National debt climbed, coming close once again to 180 percent of GDP in 1934.[42] The downturn was met by taking money out of the economy via cuts in government spending, which fed into the Treasury's attitude to the naval estimates. This led first to proposals for small – hence cheap – battleships with 12-inch guns. That in turn framed the British approach to a new naval limitation treaty when discussions began in 1935. By this time it was clear that 12-inch guns were politically unacceptable to other nations, but the British now hoped to restrict calibre to 14-inch for cost reasons. Initial sketch designs for the new battleships therefore included that possibility.[43]

For all that, the navy estimates had slowly climbed during the early 1930s and in 1934 stood at £57 million, up on previous years and with better buying power than the £58 million estimates of 1923.[44] However, that had to be framed around the general industrial decline and the fact that money was not available to quickly expand the infrastructure. Into this came a further iteration of the treaty system. The first of Britain's new generation of battleships – the *King George V* class[45] - were built to displacement and main armament restrictions defined by the Naval Limitation Treaty, also known as the Second London Naval Treaty, signed on 25 March 1936.[46]

What nobody imagined, however, was just how the interaction between Britain's severe industrial, financial and political limits, with the new treaty, was going to affect the way these battleships actually emerged – not just in terms of their technical character, but even down to the number actually built.

CHAPTER TWO
Industrial constraints

Britain faced a crippling array of limitations that framed the development of their new battleships from the mid-1930s. The restrictions of the Second London Naval Treaty were but one of the problems. Industrial limitations, financial strictures and the ongoing limits of the scale of supporting infrastructure all played a part, as did shortages of trained draftsmen. Timing and chance also played a part in the way these battleships emerged, an issue further framed by diplomatic intransigence. They were, in short, subject to a complex and inter-linked array of constraints across a range of levels.

Against all these factors, the fact that in the end these ships did virtually everything the British asked of them – and were broadly as capable overall as any other ship in the same displacement class – has been somewhat lost. The problem at the time was the appearance; 14-inch guns made the *King George V*'s the least powerful new-generation battleships of the day. And they had other operational shortcomings, including poor range and an air conditioning system that was initially not up to tropical service. A Board of Admiralty requirement for zero-elevation forward fire from A-turret meant they had minimal bow flare, which combined with freeboard limitations to make them wet in any seaway. Early war experience was dogged with mechanical problems in the gun mountings, and they had issues with watertight trunking, generator placement and details of the torpedo defence system that contributed to the loss of HMS *Prince of Wales* to air attack in 1941.[47]

The net result has been that this class have received the proverbial 'bad rap' historically. Such an impression, inevitably, is not strictly true. Indeed, some of the criticism – including the claim that they were weakly armoured amidships and vulnerable because of their aircraft hangars – was unfounded. This appears to have originated with Churchill and was debunked at the time by the First Sea Lord.[48] The reality was that the Director of Naval Construction (DNC) Sir Arthur Johns and his successor Sir Stanley Goodall, along with their teams – and particularly the battleship designer Herbert Pengelly - knew what they were doing. The main challenge was finding the best compromises needed to meet conflicting limitations that ran well beyond the Treaty limits of the day.

The fact that the design featured 14-inch guns was a consequence of politics. Although early plans explored 15-inch main armament,[49] the likelihood of a 14-inch limit was part of government thinking, and preliminary designs produced by the DNC's department in August 1935 featured that calibre in case it was confirmed.[50] The idea was that the reduction in bore could be made up for by an increase in the number of barrels – which, among other things, also meant higher chances of hitting. The problem was fitting that into the displacement limit, while still meeting the armour, range, sea-keeping needs, and other requirements the Board thought necessary. By the late 1930s it was clear that any new battleships were going to have to be capable of at least 27-28 knots.

The result was a juggling match in which the DNC's department had to meet an exacting list of specifications provided by the Board of Admiralty, all within not just the Treaty displacement, but also the dimensional limits imposed by Britain's ageing dockyard infrastructures and harbours. Parameters included optimising the armour for intended battle ranges of 12-16,000 yards.[51] This protection, in turn, was specified in part on the back of ongoing inter-war tests, including live-fire exercises against mock-ups of the proposed 'G3' armour, and others against the old super-dreadnought *Monarch*.[52] Other full-scale engineering tests suggested ways of improving protection against bombs and torpedoes,[53] and all these lessons were taken on board.

One way to save weight was by clustering the guns, an approach already taken by the French who adopted quad mountings for their *Dunkerque* class laid down in 1932.⁵⁴ The main down-sides – complex engineering, coupled with the fact that a significant proportion of armament might be eliminated by a single hit – were outweighed, literally, by the weight of such a system versus a ship with twin or even triple turrets. By early March 1936, Pengelly had a design that was 450 tons over the treaty limit with a dozen 14-inch guns in three quad mountings.⁵⁵ Curiously, US designers on the other side of the Atlantic had come up with the same arrangement for their equivalent battleship, the *North Carolina*. ⁵⁶

Into this mix now intruded the 'escalator' clause. It was clear by this time that Japan would not ratify the treaty, but for reasons of diplomatic credibility neither Britain nor the US could commit to 16-inch guns ahead of the deadline, and both needed to get their new ships started. Technically, it was possible to design the ship in such a way that the quad 14-inch mounts could be swapped for three triple 16-inch during construction. However, doing so carried weight penalties which in turn forced compromises elsewhere on displacement-limited ships. US naval planners accepted those for their *North Carolina* class, which were consequently up-gunned to 16-inch during construction.⁵⁷ The DNC looked into building similar capacity into the *King George V*,⁵⁸ but discovered it would mean altering the citadel length and weights, quite apart from the delays involved in designing new 16-inch mountings, and the idea was rejected.⁵⁹

That issue of delay in mounting design, however, reared its head late in the design process when the Board decided to further improve *King George V*'s armour and anti-torpedo protection. As finalised, the over-magazine deck protection was thought good against the 16-inch 2,375 lb shells being prepared for the *Lion* class, at a range of 30,625 yards.⁶⁰ However, among other alterations, two guns had to be dropped from the main armament to compensate for the weight. That meant designing a new twin turret, which was accepted despite the shortage of trained draftsmen. As Churchill put it, the consequence was time: the 'two or three thousand parts' that formed the 'wonderful mechanism' of the gun mountings had to be re-designed, with a 'further delay of at least a year' in completion of the first two ships.⁶¹ The fact this decision was taken irrespective of that delay underscores the way the British were prioritising protection over both offensive capacity and the initial availability of their new battleships.

The other consequence of this late design revision was reduced freeboard. That had implications for seakeeping because the ships had only five feet of sheer forwards, necessary to meet a Board requirement for zero-elevation ahead fire from A-turret.[62] Inevitably the ships ended up with a higher service displacement than designed; and one outcome of all these factors was that the *King George V* class were very wet forward. Curiously, the limiting factor in the original design was the weight and structure associated with B-turret, which had to be high enough to superfire over A.[63] If A-turret was raised to clear a significant shear-line forward, B-turret would have had to be even higher – adding weight that pushed the ships over the treaty displacement limit. Although a side point, the issue reveals just how closely interlinked ship characteristics were: even a minor re-think in one area could easily provoke changes elsewhere.

Another service problem flowed from a 1936 decision to cut fuel capacity from 4000 to 3700 tons.[64] On the basis of expected performance, this was not thought likely to reduce the unrefuelled range; but it did, for reasons that only became obvious in operations. The British had developed an anti-torpedo system that sandwiched liquid-loaded compartments with void spaces. It saved displacement to load the liquid spaces with fuel rather than water. The tanks had to be kept liquid-loaded for the system to remain effective, but in theory, it was possible to allow sea-water to enter from the bottom as fuel was pumped from the top, keeping the tanks full. The components were – theoretically – isolated and prevented from mixing by a layer of detergent. The practical problem was that under normal ship movement the oil-detergent boundary produced an emulsion layer, and the only way to stop that from clogging the feed systems and causing the superheaters to fail was to stop drawing from the tank.[65] Because liquid-loading was integral to the anti-torpedo protection, the problem could not be cured. In the end, some of the double-bottom spaces had to be converted to fuel oil tanks, cutting the effectiveness of the under-bottom protection.

Financial limits produced another key engineering constraint. The need to keep costs contained prevented the British using high-tensile armour steel – 'Ducol' or 'D' steel in Admiralty parlance – as extensively as they wanted, although it was applied to key structures such as the weather deck over the magazines and machinery spaces, and in the torpedo defence system.[66] Even so, the new battleships came in with a cost that has been variously stated, but came to around £7.4 million each,[67] of which some £1.425 million was for the armour alone.[68] The total cost was superficially cheaper than the preceding *Nelson* class, but in inflation-corrected terms it made them the most expensive capital ships yet built by Britain, and by a significant margin. To give that perspective we have to consider how economies work, and particularly the way that prices change over time. Usually they inflate, meaning that money loses value: and this compounds as inflation continues. Targeting inflation to control that loss of value did not begin until the 1990s.

In specific, and using the consumers' price index as an 'average' expression of British monetary value-change over time, one pound sterling in 1936, when *King George V* was ordered, was the approximate equivalent of £67.60 in 2018.[69] This was due in large part to a period of significant inflation after the Second World War, and particularly through into the 1960s and 1970s. By this measure, a *King George V* would have cost about £500 million in 2018 terms. However, the comparison is not exact because, aside from the way that the CPI is an 'average of averages' relative to prices of specific items, the *nature* of what can be bought with that money also changes over such time-spans, particularly in terms of military technologies.

Into this mix has to be added the fact that military technology has progressively become more expensive in real (inflation-corrected) terms across the whole industrial period. While specific measures of changing value across time are difficult to precisely calculate for a variety of reasons, the fact that Britain's Type 45 *Daring* class anti-air war destroyers, which began entering service in 2009, were procured for around £1.05 thousand million per ship ⊠ including amortising the development costs[70] – making them about twice the price of a *King George V* in 'real' terms, despite being only about a quarter of the displacement – underscores the broad point.

From the historical point of view, however, the more meaningful financial comparison is with what Britain had built previously. At the time the first *King George V*'s were ordered, the last battleships were the preceding *Nelson* class. This pair had been ordered in December 1922, and *Nelson* was built for just over £7.5 million.[71] Because Britain was in effective recession from 1921 until the Second World War, average prices *fell* by an average of 1.8 percent annually between 1921 and 1936; the country was suffering deflation.

If we take compound deflation between 1922 and 1936 out of the calculation – in other words, calculating the 'real' ('inflation-corrected') value using 1936 price levels as a baseline, the estimated cost of a 1922-era 'G3' was around £5.16 million in 1936 terms.[72] This was materially *less* than the cost of the *King George V* class. And yet the cost of defence procurement kept rising, because if we reverse the baseline and calculate the cost of a *King George V* in 1922 values, we find it would have cost around £10.74 million in that money,[73] making the ship more expensive in equivalent value terms than the ⊠G3⊠ class which had been budgeted at £9 million per unit in 1921.

The point of all these comparisons is to underscore the fact that, given Britain's ongoing financial issues, the decision to embark on a major battleship programme in 1936 was very significant, both politically and financially. Given the huge cost of the new ships, the compromises the Admiralty then had to make in order to keep the costs down as far as possible were essential. In point of fact, these ships were only part of a significant build-up of the period that included all classes of vessel, emphasising the financial constraints confronted by the battleships.

The only point over which there was no compromise was the fact that new battleships were needed as part of the mix. Nobody knew the future, and in the late 1930s battleships remained a key arbiter of sea force and a measure of naval strength that still had political significance at a time when the international situation was deteriorating. There was war between Japan and China. A fascist-led Italy was flexing its muscles in North Africa. Germany was on the rise once again, this time as an extremist police-state version of its Imperial incarnation of the First World War. The Soviet Union was not merely ideologically opposed to the west but was also another extremist police state under the thumb of its paranoid dictator, Joseph Stalin.

The major western democracies of the day – a group essentially reduced to Britain, France and the United States – were still on their economic knees as a result of the great depression; and although the United States had immense latent industrial and economic power, they remained isolationist; and the potential of democracy to prevail as a significant world ideology was not clear. This point is often lost amidst the fact that the Allies won the Second World War, but in the 1930s the outcome of the political oppositions was unknown and, as a result, the rising power of the totalitarian states – both fascist and communist – was alarming.

The naval aspect was given intensity by the fact that the Anglo-German Naval Agreement of June 1935 permitted Germany to build a fleet up to 35 percent the size of Britain's, albeit with ships theoretically restricted by existing treaty limitations. Italy, who had become Germany's fascist ally, was also embarking on a battleship building programme, also ostensibly within the treaty limits. The issue here, aside from the potential of cheating, was that new ships able to challenge the balance of power were clearly on the way. Meanwhile, Japan – which was effectively run by a militarist junta and had ambitions of its own in Asia - had renounced all treaty obligations.

This again threw focus on the limitations the British faced when contemplating battleship programmes. British naval plans, formally approved in January 1936,[74] projected 10 new capital ships to be laid down by 1940-41 in annual programmes on a 2-3-2-2-1 frequency.[75] This was later adjusted to add a second battleship to the 1940 programme.[76] All this was part of a more general British naval re-armament which led to a rise in naval building costs from £10.2 million in 1934 to £46.1 million in 1939. The bulk of the rise was from 1937.[77] However, as projected in 1936, the battleship plan in particular was always going to be difficult to achieve given the industrial and financial limitations involved. Nor was this the only restriction. A significant technical problem in 1936 was that Article 4 of the second part of the Second London Naval Treaty restricted battleships to 14-inch guns on 35,000 tons standard displacement.[78] All this was signalled well ahead of time, meaning that designers both in Britain and the US were preparing for it,[79] and was why the *King George V* class, the first two of which were laid down under the 1936 programme, were armed with 14-inch guns.[80]

The same clause allowed main armament to revert to 16-inch if any of the original signatories of the 'Washington Treaty' of 1922 failed to ratify the new arrangement by 1 April 1937.[81] The Japanese were not expected to do so, but despite British diplomatic efforts to obtain an early answer, Japan would not openly admit the point ahead of deadline.[82] The British issue was that thanks largely to budgetary deadlines and the lead-times required for heavy naval weapons, they had to order their three 1937-programme battleships by late 1936.[83] In absence of an early Japanese answer, this meant confirming three repeats of the *King George V* class.[84] Japan refused to ratify when the time came in April 1937,[85] but by then it was too late.

As a result of this combination of national moral integrity, timing, and capacity limitations, the British ended up building five *King George V*s, which became their only new battleships to serve during the Second World War. Perhaps the biggest issue involved the main armament. This came under heavy criticism as soon as the Admiralty committed to it: the 14-inch guns were smaller than those of any other new capital ships of the day

19

with the exception of the *Dunkerque* class, which had 13-inch guns, and the *Scharnhorst* class, which had 11.1-inch.[86]

The most trenchant critique came from Churchill, who as former First Lord of the Admiralty had a lasting enthusiasm for the territory. His warnings about the totalitarian powers had given him the repute of being a warmonger; and while he had his friends in the service, he was not slow to criticise what he felt were poor decisions. The Admiralty, he insisted, would look 'rather silly' if they committed to 14-inch ships when both the US and Japan might then build 16-inch. Furthermore, he declared – following Lord Fisher – that the British navy 'always travels first class'.[87] His critique struck a chord. The First Lord, Sir Samuel Hoare, responded; if the heavy gun mountings and turrets for the *King George V* class had not been ordered in April 1936, ahead of the Japanese withdrawal from the treaty system, Britain would have only two new battleships available by 1941.[88]

As events panned out, this was true in any case; but that point was not obvious when this exchange took place. Churchill never resiled from his criticism of the new class. He was comforted by news that the *King George V*'s had a dozen 14-inch guns, not nine – 'a considerable improvement in weight of metal'. However, he later considered that the reduction to ten guns meant that his objections about their inferiority to 16-inch armed ships 'resumed their force'.[89]

Was this criticism valid? To the extent that none of the new battleships had been tested in combat when he raised his objections, it was. However, the paper performance of their main armament – a new design of all-steel construction - was broadly comparable with the older Mk I 15-inch/42 calibre gun that armed the bulk of the British battle-fleet in 1939, and superior to them in some respects.[90] These design figures were borne out in action. When *King George V* joined *Rodney* in the final cannonade against *Bismarck*, her 14-inch shells were observed to be effective alongside *Rodney*'s in destroying the fighting capacity of the German battleship, including by penetrating heavy armour such as the conning tower.[91] This was a short-range battle; but when *Duke of York* took on *Scharnhorst* at the end of 1943, there was also no question about the effectiveness of British 14-inch fire at long range, where *Duke of York*'s shells penetrated *Scharnhorst*'s citadel armour, disabling her propulsion machinery.[92] The curious point is that *Scharnhorst* was more heavily armoured than *Bismarck*.[93] Later, when *King George V* was bombarding targets on Honshu in July 1945, her 14-inch guns were as effective on ground targets as any other. This was also the last time a British battleship fired its guns at an enemy.[94]

For all that, the new 14-inch guns and its mountings had many problems. One serious issue was the fact that the quad mountings were significantly wider than previous twin and triple turrrets, and the structures supporting the revolving sections tended to flex as the hull worked in certain sea conditions. That stopped the turrets training at times. The other key problem was that the guns were designed for all-round loading, requiring a handling room with a revolving hoist. All had to be flash-proof, and the below-decks mechanisms tended to jam as a result of over-tight tolerance and structural flexing from normal ship movement.[95]

All this was correctable given time. Indeed, so-called 'teething problems' of this kind were typical of any new design. The *Nelson* class had their own share of issues with their triple 16-inch mountings on completion in the late 1920s, which took some years to resolve – it was not until 1934 that *Nelson* was able to fire all guns in a 16-round firing sequence without breakdowns, and even then the class had occasional issues.[96] What brought the *King George V*'s problems into relief was the fact that the ships were thrown into war without a period in which to correct mechanical matters. The main difficulties with the armament were eventually corrected – for the earlier ships in the class during refit, and for the later as a modification during construction. Even then, however, issues continued to crop up, including during *Duke of York*'s engagement with *Scharnhorst*.[97]

In general, as war experience underscored, the *King George V*'s were as good in practical service as any other treaty-limited battleship of the same period. The main point of comparison is the US Navy's equivalent battleship, the *North Carolina* class. They were close contemporaries of the *King George V* and built to the same treaty specification. The original designs for both even featured similar main armament: a dozen 14-inch guns in quad mountings, backed with armour thought adequate by their respective administrations – bearing in mind that US armour requirements were less than those of the British – and similar maximum sea speeds of around 27-28 knots. The differences came about because of varying design philosophies, coupled with the fact that the timings relative to ordering deadlines were a little different – and the fact that the United States had materially superior financial and industrial resources.

The most obvious difference in the final designs was that the US ships were armed with 16-inch guns. As we have seen, however, this was a consequence of the fact that the British were not prepared to compromise the *King George V* design to create the option of up-gunning during construction, coupled with the delays consequent on developing designs for 16-inch mountings.

In any event, it was still a case of swings and roundabouts. Both classes were also designed as relatively fast battleships with similar horsepower: 110,000 in the British case and 121,000 in the US.[98] This produced generally similar sea speeds. *North Carolina* had a practical sea speed of 27-28 knots, as against the *King George V*'s practical speed of a little over 28.[99] But the differences were immaterial. Where the *North Carolina* excelled was in propulsion plant efficiency and range; the US vessel employed a steam plant built around double-reduction gears and relatively high-pressure steam systems, pioneered in the USS *Mahan* of 1933.[100] This offered superior power-to-weight ratio and better fuel efficiency than the 'Admiralty' three-drum boilers the British employed for the *King George V*'s. American crew habitability standards were also significantly superior to the British. And the US Navy was able to make more extensive use of high-tensile steel on the back of better budgets, which gave their ships a significant structural edge.

There were greater differences in armour design, and not simply because the American battleship was designed with an immunity zone optimised against 14-inch fire; whereas the *King George V*'s had a good immunity zone against 16-inch. There were also significant differences in the philosophy behind their protective systems. The US battleship carried side armour on a 15-degree inward sloping belt, which improved resistance and meant a lighter belt could be carried for the same protection.[101] By contrast, British thinking had swung away from this system by the 1930s and back to a heavy vertical external belt. This improved the volume of protected hull and increased the reserve buoyancy of the citadel. However, that was not the key factor behind the decision; in fact, the reversion to a heavy vertical belt was primarily due to concerns, based on tests, that shell fragments could be deflected to pass below a sloped internal armour system, particularly as the ship moved in a seaway.[102] The other down-sides of sloped armour – the technical difficulty of repairing an internal armoured belt, along with asymmetric flooding if the shell plating was damaged, outboard of the belt – were also concerns, but of less concern than the risk of fragment penetration.

Again, such a decision for designers was a question of balancing advantages and risks in order to meet the specifications of the naval authorities: designers on both sides of the Atlantic were well aware of the engineering issues. In the event, neither the US nor the British armour systems were properly tested in battle. *Prince of Wales*' May 1941 engagement with *Bismarck* lasted only a few minutes;[103] and in November 1942, *Washington* destroyed the 14-inch gunned *Kirishima*'s fighting power so swiftly that the Japanese could not effectively fight back.[104] During *Bismarck*'s final battle, *King George V* was not hit at all;[105] and *Duke of York* – although well protected against *Scharnhorst*'s 11.1-inch guns – was only hit by splinters and a 5.9-inch shell that did superficial damage during the Battle of North Cape.[106]

What all this meant was that, in general, the first US and British 'Treaty' battleship types built after the 'holiday' ended were essentially variations on a similar theme – and understandably so. While there were many differences in specifics, in general there was little to choose between the industrial technologies of the various battleship-building nations, and for the good reason. All were subject to the exact same laws of physics, notably those of ballistics, metallurgy and fluid dynamics. Differing design philosophies, particular staff requirements, and even differences in specific technology - as we have seen relative to *King George V* and *North Carolina* – shifted the balance, but in terms of overall military capability, broadly defined by a combination of offensive and defensive power, speed, range, crew habitability and factors such as ability to achieve defined performance in certain load or fouling conditions, a meaningful advantage could only be gained through significant shifts in displacement. This was well understood at the time and, indeed, was why displacement had been identified as the key limit in the treaty system from the outset.

So why were the *King George V* class given the proverbial 'bad rap'? Part of the answer is the fact that the popular definition of battleship power, then and since, was the calibre of the main armament. In an era when 16-inch weapons were the norm, Britain's 14-inch guns superficially didn't seem to cut it. As we have seen, this was essentially a consequence of their penury and industrial capacity, coupled with timing – three distinct limiting factors that came together. To this has to be added the fact that these battleships were a new design, innovating in many ways in an engineering sense, yet had to immediately enter some of the most intense fighting of the war at sea to that time. The results highlighted engineering and technical issues that, in peacetime, would have been resolved without great drama.

CHAPTER THREE
The lure of second hand guns

The limitations Britain faced when it came to a major battleship programme by the late 1930s were underscored by the way that the Admiralty had to find creative answers when developing programmes to meet the strategic challenges emerging by that time. Totalitarianism was gaining ground in Europe, driven by Germany and its ally Italy. War flared in China from 1937, where Japan engaged in a major campaign that included a remarkable outburst of violence in the nationalist Chinese capital, Nanking.

British efforts to re-arm were genuinely intended, but by any practical measure dilatory against the pace of these international developments. It was understandable in a way: naval construction was always a multi-year affair. That was especially so for battleships. The issue of gun calibre resolved itself by April 1937 with Japan's refusal to ratify the Second London Naval Treaty. Although compelled by timing to order an additional three *King George V* class battleships for their 1937 programme, the Admiralty were determined to push ahead with 16-inch gunned battleships for the 1938 programme.

The challenge was that these ships were also expected to be limited to 35,000 tons. Although often conflated with the subsequent increase in displacement to 45,000 tons – even in significant reference works[107] – the 'escalator' clause of the Second London Naval Treaty of 1936 referred only to main armament.[108] In practise, it also only affected the British and United States. The French were committed to 15-inch gunned ships designed in 1934-35 under terms of the original London Naval Treaty, which allowed up to 16-inch weapons. The first of two, *Richielieu*, was laid down in 1935 under terms of that Treaty. The French were signatories to the Second London Naval Treaty, but by the time two more battleships were ordered in 1938,[109] the 'escalator clause' had been invoked. The Italians, similarly, were building 15-inch gunned ships under terms of the original London Naval Treaty;[110] as were Germany, who coat-tailed on those provisions via the June 1935 Anglo-German Naval agreement.[111] The fact that the latter two were flouting the displacement limits was suspected, but could not be proven.

In theory, all these ships could be generally matched by the *King George V* and *North Carolina* classes. The *King George V*, particularly, had an excellent immunity zone against 15-inch fire; and *North Carolina* had higher firepower than the European vessels.[112] Japan's declared intentions were another matter, although the actual outcome of their policies was obfuscated by Japanese diplomats, who disingenuously implied that any new ships might be 40,000 tons.[113] Both the United States and Britain believed that Japan's new ships would be at least 43,000 tons,[114] an estimate that underscores the extent to which Japan managed to hide its actual activities. In fact they built battleships displacing a third more than this figure.

In pedantic terms, of course, even Britain and the United States did not *precisely* build 35,000 ton battleships. *King George V* was signed off at 35,500 tons in the expectation of weight saving during construction. The standard displacement was also calculated with a reduced number of stowed shells; there was room for more.[115] Weights calculated in September 1936 produced a standard displacement of 36,916 tons. Despite calls for weight saving during construction – driven as much by engineering as legal needs after April 1937 – the name-ship was completed at 36,727 tons standard.[116] Curiously, the *North Carolina*'s official 1942 standard displacement was virtually identical at 36,600 tons,[117] although a 1941 weight summary put her 'light ship' condition at 35,102 tons and standard displacement with ammunition, crew, supplies and aircraft at 38,004 tons.[118]

The differences underscore the fact that ship weights always varied, usually depending on loading, something that the treaty agreements tried to define, but not always successfully. However, none of this was material when compared with the way the Germans – for example – explicitly flouted the agreed standard displacement by more than 15 percent in their *Bismarck* class.[119]

For all that, none of the democracies were prepared to blatantly break their own treaty limits. Reasons included the need to honour the integrity of international diplomacy and with it international agreements ranging from trade arrangements to the treatment of prisoners during war. However, the displacement differential between the expected new Japanese vessels – as anticipated by the west in the late 1930s - and the older treaty limit was not so great as to create an insurmountable disparity in fighting power, providing the 35,000 ton designs were carefully optimised.

As a result, during 1937 both Britain and the United States focussed on 16-inch gunned, 35,000 ton fast battleships with suitable immunity zones against their own main armament. Both nations had something of a head start: they had already looked into this when developing their 1936 designs.[120] In Britain,[121] that work indicated that a 16-inch gunned version could not be built to meet specific Admiralty needs within the 35,000 ton limit.[122] Complications included the fact that the Admiralty felt that heavier side armour than *King George V*'s would be needed to improve the 16-inch immunity zone, but the necessary plates – 16.5 or 17 inches thick – were still under development and the first experimental examples would not be ready until 1938.[123]

Later in 1937, Pengelly showed that if certain compromises were made, a 16-inch battleship with good protection and adequate speed was – *just* – possible within the limit.[124] But the compromises were severe, including reduced area of armour, reductions in secondary armament, and aircraft capacity slashed back to a turret-top catapult. At the time, aircraft were thought essential for spotting long-range fall of shot. The first version, dubbed '16A-38', was swiftly overtaken by a revision, '16B-38', which repeated the *King George V* propulsion on request of the Engineer-in-Chief,[125] Vice-Admiral George Preece.[126] A further version followed with the secondary armament cut down still further.[127]

Studies of a similar ship on the other side of the Atlantic were more fruitful, in part because US Navy staff requirements differed from those of the Admiralty. There were also differences in technique. The United States, for example, retained inclined internal side armour.[128] This offered significant weight-savings, at the cost of reserve buoyancy and potential for asymmetric flooding outside the armour. The outcome was the four-strong *South Dakota* class.[129] These ships, too, carried compromises, notably in terms of a compact superstructure that led to blast interference in the secondary armament. By the time they were approaching completion in the early 1940s, they were also felt to be too slow to work with aircraft carriers. However, they were perhaps the best of the Treaty-limited battleships, combining adequate speed with an excellent main armament, without compromising protection or unrefuelled range.[130]

In the event, the British fiscal and construction timetable was different from that of the US Navy's, and the Admiralty did not order their *South Dakota* analogue for their two-ship 1938 programme. Instead, the design was overtaken by a revision of the treaty displacement. This came at United States insistence and was predictable given the political situation in Asia,[131] combined with the practical problems of building a balanced 16-inch gunned fast battleship on 35,000 tons. Staff requirements on both sides of the Atlantic included specified range, crew habitability, sea-keeping, stability, underwater defence and a multitude of other factors including arcs of fire. Being able to achieve defined speeds at certain load conditions and after certain times out of dock also played a part, among other requirements.

As we have seen, 16-inch gunned fast battleships to the 35,000 ton limit were possible, in part by compromising staff requirements; but they were not thought optimal in the longer term. By 1937, the US Navy was particularly concerned by the 27.5-knot design speed of both the *North Carolinas* and *South Dakotas*, fast by earlier standards, but now thought insufficient for projected fleet work.[132] Questions were raised as to whether the *North Carolinas* – already under construction – could be re-designed for 30 knots, and whether four 27.5-knot *South Dakotas* should be ordered.[133]

In the end all six battleships went ahead as planned, and the US Navy's Bureau of Construction and Repair instead began contemplating higher speed battleships for which initial sketches, completed in early 1938, began with a displacement of just over 49,000 tons standard. Other plans were drawn up for slower battleships with a dozen 16-inch guns, essentially four-turret versions of *South Dakota*, which were also going to be over the treaty limit.[134]

All these exercises made clear that further United States construction was going to need higher displacement. The Second London Naval treaty had provision to negotiate new parameters,[135] and after calls from Washington, discussions between Britain, France and the United States began on 31 March 1938.[136] On the basis of their design studies, United States negotiators were looking for at least 45,000 tons. This caused alarm in the Admiralty because, as the First Sea Lord, Admiral of the Fleet Sir Ernle Chatfield,[137] pointed out, any ship with beam over 110 feet – which the combination of Britain's 1930s requirements and 45,000 ton displacement implied – could not be docked in home yards.[138] The Admiralty wanted to keep limits to around 40,000 tons for this reason but felt that they could, if pushed, accept 43,000.[139]

These negotiations were informed by ongoing design work on both sides of the Atlantic.[140] American designers, for instance, produced four possible 45,000 ton 'fast battleship' sketches in April 1938.[141] The British, meanwhile, explored options within their own infrastructure limits. One outcome was Design 16F-38, initially 39,000 tons standard, but incremented up to 40,000, with similar speed to *King George V*, nine 16-inch guns and a dozen 5.25-inch secondary weapons. The DNC's department also sketched a variant, Design 16G-38, which included a specification to reach design endurance under tropical conditions, and was capable of 30 knots on 43,000 tons. An alternative with reduced power could still achieve 28.5 knots on 41,000 tons.[142] Sketches were also produced for a 48,500 ton ship with a dozen 16-inch guns. As D. K. Brown observes, this work served to reinforce the earlier belief that, for Britain, the largest practical battleship they could build by this time was closer to 40,000 tons standard.[143]

Britain was, in short, running into yet another of the many limits consequent on their long decline since the late Victorian period, and particularly during the inter-war years. In the end they had to bend to US demands for 45,000 tons. A diplomatic protocol was signed to that effect on 30 June.[144] This confirmed the new treaty displacement, to which the US Navy's high-speed battleships, the *Iowas*, were then built.[145] The British still had to build closer to 40,000 tons because of infrastructure limits,[146] and the DNC's department used 16F-38 as the basis for further development during June 1938. This became the *Lion* class. The final design produced a ship similar in concept to *King George V*, but with nine 16-inch guns, transom stern and higher design speed. That could be achieved with a standard displacement of around 40,550 tons. The first two, *Lion* and *Temeraire*, were ordered in February 1939, and laid down mid-year.[147]

Despite a jump in size and fire-power, however, the new battleships were related to the preceding *King George V*'s, with much the same general layout and protection scheme.[148] The main difference was in the armament; the 16-inch guns were of an new all-steel design, in the same family as the 14-inch of the *King George V* class – both of which derived from a 12-inch steel gun developed in the early 1930s - and very different from the Mk I 16-inch guns fitted to the *Nelsons*.[149] In particular, the new model 16-inch reverted to the heavy-shell, modest muzzle velocity combination that had made Britain's main naval guns of the First World War era so successful.[150]

This family relationship between warship designs was not unusual in British naval circles; once a concept had been worked out, subsequent designs were often improvements rather than radical re-thinking.[151] The 'dreadnought' naval race of 1906-14 had been a classic example, ultimately producing a run of a dozen very similar 13.5-inch gunned 'super-dreadnoughts', starting with the the *Orion* class laid down in 1909-10.[152] Other ships designed in British yards, such as the *Reshadieh*, were generally similar. The 'family' similarities of the broader concepts were also clear, and understandably so for ships designed and laid down in quick succession.[153] Similarly, the jump from *King George V* to *Lion* was not exceptional in terms of the underlying concepts driving both types.

Two *Lion* class battleships – *Lion* and *Temeraire* –were authorised under the 1938 programme for laying down in 1939.[154] Two more were projected for the 1939 programme.[155] In the event, of course, none came to fruition. Only the 1938 and 1939 programme ships were authorised before war intervened. Of these, just three were formally ordered and only two laid down before war broke out.[156] The fourth ship, *Conqueror*, was assigned a yard number – 567 – which was used, ultimately, for *Vanguard*.[157]

None of the *Lions* were ever finished. The arbiter of their demise was the outbreak of war and, with it, a reallocation of priorities. The fact that they were authorised, ordered and then begun remains tantalising. Would the first two *Lions*, at least, have seen service had war not broken out in 1939? Given the circumstances of the late 1930s, it is difficult to see war between Germany, France and Britain being deferred far beyond the moment when it actually broke out. German dictator Adolf Hitler had been leading Europe towards war by ever-bolder steps since the middle of the decade. Partly on the basis of the British 'appeasement' policy, he apparently believed he could avert conflict with the major powers until he chose. Certainly he did not expect his brinksmanship over Poland in August-September 1939 to provoke war with France and Britain.

In fact, the western democracies were not as supine as Hitler presumed and the likelihood of avoiding war in the face of Hitler's belligerence was low. Poland was the litmus test, and it was not something Hitler could back away from because he had already made arrangements to split the nation with his ally-of-convenience, the Soviet Union. Given the general conduct of the Nazi regime, coupled with the hardening resolve of the democracies, it seems likely that Europe would have been at war by 1940, one way or another. Given the way British naval programmes were revised to meet war needs, coupled with the way they evolved towards aviation vessels on the back of war experiences, the fate of the *Lions* if war broke out in late 1940 would likely still been suspension and then cancellation. To suppose a still later outbreak demands a more unlikely sequence of events involving other changed assumptions back into the mid-1930s, at which point issues arise as to counter-factual options associated with the 1936 naval treaty.

Exactly how many of *Lions* might ultimately have been built is speculative. The battleship programme confirmed in 1936, to which the Admiralty was still operating when war broke out, called for two battleships to be ordered in 1938, two in 1939 and one in 1940.[158] By some accounts up to six *Lions* were projected,[159] evidently on the expectation of a second ship being authorised in the 1940 programme. But this again ran into the limits of Britain's industrial capacity. The immediate constraint was the number of heavy gun mountings that could be built; and in 1938-39, national capacity was seven triple 16-inch mountings annually, meaning Britain could commit to two ships a year.[160] That made a second ship in the 1940 programme possible. However, whether the 1940 programme would have featured *Lions*, or an 'improved' variant – is moot. Standard British practise to that time had been to mildly amend warship designs across multi-year procurements.

The Admiralty's main problem in early 1939 was that despite every effort to bring their 1936 programme to reality, the world situation continued to deteriorate, and did so faster than the new battleships could be completed. By this time five *King George V*'s were under construction, with the first two due to complete in 1940-41. Two *Lions* were about to be laid down and two more had been confirmed under the 1939 programme for laying down in 1940. However, the Admiralty now felt this programme was insufficient to match Japan, Germany and Italy together.[161] The bottleneck was the capacity of the British arms industry to build heavy gun mountings. It was thought possible to expand production to ten such mountings annually, which would permit a third 16-inch ship in the 1940 programme; but that required infrastructure work at the former Harland and Wolff Scotstoun Ordnance Works.[162]

There were, however, other possibilities. Four twin Mk I 15-inch/42 calibre mountings, built in 1915-17 for the 'large light cruisers' *Courageous* and *Glorious*,[163] had not been scrapped when the cruisers were converted to aircraft carriers during the 1920s.[164] Instead they remained in storage at Devonport.[165] The possibility of using these mountings on a new-build hull had been raised in April 1937.[166] At that time the concept did not get very far; the DNC's department produced sketch designs of a *King George V* with six or eight 15-inch weapons.[167] The main focus of Admiralty attention in 1937 was on finding ways of squeezing 16-inch guns along with all the other desired characteristics into battleship of 35,000 tons. But by 1939, with risk of war made all the more real for the British government and its officials by the Munich crisis, the idea re-surfaced. It was also clear that further 15-inch mountings were going to become available as the *Revenge* class battleships were scrapped.[168]

There seemed potential for such a vessel in the Far East,[169] where Britain had built a major regional naval base in Singapore as part of a strategic effort to defend Australia and New Zealand along with Britain's own interests in the area, but where it might be difficult to provide reinforcements if war was already under way in Europe.

The idea of re-using older weapons again highlighted the limits Britain faced in terms of its arms-construction capacity; but it was not considered a huge disadvantage. The Vickers Mk I 15-inch/42 calibre naval gun was an outstanding weapon when first deployed in 1915,[170] offering excellent hitting power and range by First World War standards, coupled with superb accuracy and low bore wear.[171] By the 1930s this gun had been surpassed in many aspects.[172] But while it lacked the range or armour penetration of more recent and larger weapons,[173] other details such as muzzle velocity remained comparable with new-generation naval guns.[174] In point of fact, the armour penetration of the Mk I 15-inch/42 at certain ranges was marginally *better* than the new-generation Mk VII 14-inch/45 calibre weapons fitted to the *King George V* class.[175] It remained the primary weapon of the fleet in the 1930s, and deficiencies in range, by period standards, had been partially and variously corrected by modifying some of the Mk I mountings to 30 degree elevation, introducing more streamlined (6-crh) shells, and allowing heavier charges ('supercharges') on unmodified mountings.[176]

In Far East service, such a weapon was certainly going to be effective against the Japanese heavy cruisers, rumoured Japanese 'super-cruisers',[177] and the IJN's older capital ships, some of which had been built to British designs during the First World War.[178] A new battleship of around 40,000 tons, built to the latest concepts and with modern fire-control, was also likely to be adequate when deploying older 15-inch guns against any Japanese battleships thought to be under construction. Although rumours of very large battleships had filtered back to London, the general consensus was that the new Japanese ships would probably mount 16-inch guns on perhaps 43,000 tons standard.[179]

As projected in 1939, a battleship armed with the stored mountings could be laid down for the 1940 programme without affecting the *Lions*.[180] Cost savings were not great: the armament would have to be modernised, and the DNC estimated the cost of the new battleship would still come in at around £7 million. Running costs were another issue. Britain was still far from recovered economically, and there was talk of selling the ship to Australia.[181] The DNC's department developed initial plans incorporating similar protection to *King George V*, which had a fair immunity zone against 16-inch fire.[182] The ship was otherwise broadly a four-turret version of the 1938 *Lion*, with the same propulsion plant, transom stern, secondary and anti-aircraft armament, aviation facilities, and similar superstructure.[183] By mid-July 1939 the DNC had three options to hand for further development.[184]

All came to a halt when war broke out with Germany in early September. The Admiralty reorganised its office spaces to free room for war operations staff, and the Department of Naval Construction was sent to Bath, west of London.[185] This took the DNC out of daily contact with Admiralty staff, which hindered design development.

The war brought dramatic changes to Britain's battleship programmes as the focus shifted to more immediate war needs and away from longer-term construction. The *Lion* class were suspended on 3 October,[186] along with the final *King George V* class battleship *Howe*.[187] In the event, *Howe* was shortly resumed, and launched on 9 April 1940.[188] But while work on the *Lions* also resumed, progress was desultory and by the time they were halted for a second time in May 1940, only 218 tons of steel had been assembled for

Lion and 121 for *Temeraire*.[189]

But there was another option. When war broke out, battleships remained the prime arbiter of sea force, and Britain had no new ships to hand; *King George V* was not due to complete until December and the second of class, *Prince of Wales*, not until March 1941. The other three were not due to complete until 1941-42.[190] Late in 1939, Winston Churchill – now First Lord of the Admiralty,[191] picked up the idea of using the old 15-inch mountings from a remark by the Deputy Chief of the Naval Staff, Rear-Admiral Tom Phillips.[192] In early December, he asked for a 'legend with estimates in money and time' for what he called a ship of the 'battleship-cruiser type' using these weapons. It was, he insisted, to be 'heavily armoured and absolutely proof against air attack'.[193]

The upshot was that in January 1940, the Admiralty resumed work on designs for a new battleship with second-hand guns. The ship was initially projected under the 1940 Emergency War Programme,[194] and formally added to the schedule in March.[195] Further work in early 1940 adjusted the oil capacity, and new plans were approved in May.[196] In September, however, the Vice-Chief of Naval Staff became concerned about draft in both *Lion* and *Vanguard*, which restricted harbour access. This led to 'Design 15E/1940' for *Vanguard*, with a beam of 108 feet.[197] The side armour was marginally thinned, in part to offset the weight of deck armour required for increased beam. However, standard displacement still rose to 41,900 tons with deep load of 47,500.[198]

Vanguard was officially ordered in mid-March 1941,[199] and builders plans were delivered to John Brown & Co. ten days later.[200] That week Churchill – now Prime Minister and Minister of Defence[201] – urged that the remaining *King George V*'s should be completed 'at full speed' and declared that *Vanguard*, 'the only capital ship which can reach us in 1943 and before 1945' was 'most desirable'.[202] Although improvements to the design excluded her from docks in Rosyth and Plymouth – underscoring the limits of Britain's supporting infrastructure – *Vanguard*'s new plans were approved by the Board of Admiralty in mid-April 1941.[203]

The *Lions* were still suspended and their design relatively fluid. Churchill had his concerns, at one stage urging a *Nelson* style layout because he decided that the midships hangar made them vulnerable.[204] This reflected the misconception he also had about the *King George V*'s. He was wrong: as the First Sea Lord, Sir Dudley Pound, pointed out, the 'aircraft hangars in the *King George V* class did not weaken the citadel. This had to include protection for the machinery spaces, which was enormously increased in these ships as compared with the *Nelsons'*.[205]

In point of fact, the wisdom of having aircraft aboard battleships was being questioned by this time. The advent of radar – including radar range-finders – coupled with the fact that aircraft carriers had become integral to any naval force, rendered battleship-carried spotter aircraft moot. Admiralty opinion, certainly within the DNC's department, was that the displacement and space was better used to improve the anti-aircraft armament.

The Admiralty still hoped to build the *Lion* class, and many modifications applied to *Vanguard* were included in further design revisions for *Lion* approved in 1942. However, by this time the increasing capability of aircraft, and with it the rising value of aircraft carriers, had swung the balance of opinion. The formal decision was made during a meeting on 14 September 1942 to re-focus the fleet around aircraft carriers.[206] By this time a significant light carrier programme was under way,[207] a number of which were slated for construction at the Vickers Walker facility contracted for *Lion*. That would have delayed work on *Lion* until at least 1944.[208] Then, in April 1943, the two ships in the class still authorised – *Lion* and *Temeraire* - were formally cancelled.[209]

These shifts of policy marked the effective end of Britain's battleship era; but that was not obvious to all at the time. A significant pro-battleship voice remained in the Admiralty and in a narrative sense there was still a coda to play out. While nobody could anticipate the future in detail, Germany still had two capital ships to hand. In the event, that led to Britain's last heavy ship-to-ship action at sea – the engagement between HMS *Duke of York* and the *Scharnhorst* on 26 December 1943.[210] There was also the role that the battleships of the British Pacific Fleet played in the war against Japan until August 1945.[211] And HMS *Vanguard* remained under construction.

CHAPTER FOUR
War limitations

War priorities created new limitations for the British battleship programme as the war continued. Once HMS *Howe*, last of the *King George V*'s, was formally completed on 20 August 1942,[212] *Vanguard* became the sole British battleship under construction. A substantial part of Britain's maritime construction effort by this time was going on the escort ships and merchants needed to sustain the war, backed by 'light fleet' carriers. Large-ship construction was also focused on aircraft carriers, initially the four-ship *Audacious* class, of which the first was laid down in October 1942.[213]

The decision to switch construction away from battleships was not without its critics. The Admiralty retained its pro-battleship voices – notably the incoming First Sea Lord, Admiral Sir Andrew Browne Cunningham, a fighting admiral in the tradition of Nelson whose personal leadership had done much to swing the Mediterranean war in British favour during the dark days of 1941-42.[214] There was, therefore, hope that the *Lions* might be built for the post-war fleet, and design work continued on the basis of war lessons, interspersed with options such as a hybrid battleship-carrier.[215]

Vanguard had been authorised in part because she was likely to be completed in less time than a ship that had to wait on new gun-mountings. In fact, she too fell victim to changing war needs. The battleship was laid down in October 1941 by John Brown & Co,[216] and prioritised after the loss of *Prince of Wales* and *Repulse* in December.²¹⁷ This was reflected in Churchill's plans for 1942, where he ruled out work on the two *Lion* class battleships laid down in 1939, cancelled two further *Lions* outright, cancelled four heavy cruisers from the 1940 programme, and ordered that shipyard labour should focus on repairing merchants and completing new fleet carriers.²¹⁸ The exception was *Vanguard*, which he wanted 'pressed forward' within the 'limits of the armour-plate provision' of some 16,500 tons nationally in 1941 – divided between army and navy – and 25,000 tons in 1942.²¹⁹ *Vanguard* had already been assigned constructional steel originally delivered for *Lion*.²²⁰

This was a further practical limit; at a time when Britain was building equipment for all branches of the military, both armour and mild steel had to be rationed. Another constraint was labour availability. The net result – in which *Vanguard*'s fortunes fell victim to various gyrations of war priority and available labour - was that the battleship was not launched until the end of November 1944, well after the expected service date projected when she was originally authorised.²²¹

Such dilatory progress, however, also meant there were significant design changes along the way, although the scope for change reduced as construction progressed. In July 1942 there was a proposal to convert *Vanguard* into an aircraft carrier. This was declined, apparently on the basis that the battleship-style design would render her a very mediocre carrier.²²² Particular lessons were drawn from the investigations into the loss both of *Prince of Wales* and of the cruiser *Belfast*,²²³ along with combat experience such as the battle of the Denmark Strait in May 1941. This resulted, among other things, in a requirement to add armour to *Vanguard*'s magazine sides for improved splinter protection.²²⁴

Another war lesson flowed from the practical sea-experience of the *King George V* class, which were very wet forward. This led to a decision in September 1942 to dramatically increase *Vanguard*'s sheer forward.²²⁵ The decision defeated the Admiralty requirement for zero-elevation ahead-fire, but promised to rectify the problems the *King George V* class had in even moderate swells.²²⁶ The rake had to be restricted so the ship could fit into the Devonport graving dock.²²⁷ And the discontinuity in the sheer line made it look very much the add-on it was: as R. J. Daniel observed when he saw it, the bow design was clearly a 'late change'.²²⁸

Many other adjustments, including deleting the aircraft in favour of an improved anti-aircraft battery, were included in revised plans approved in November 1942.[229] All this added weight; final design deep-load was 48,140 tons – and even that eventually fell by the wayside. The ship was completed with a deep load of 51,420 tons. This reduced the freeboard, making the bow flare even more crucial, but also affected stability and hull loadings.[230]

The 15-inch mountings were modified for *Vanguard* in the former Coventry Ordnance Works by Harland and Wolff.[231] The cost of this work was a significant part of the total cost of the battleship, some £3,186,868.[232] Technical work included adding new trunnion blocks for higher elevation.[233] Insulation and dehumidifiers were incorporated to improve working conditions for the gun crews.[234] One problem was that none of the mountings had been intended for superfiring positions, which meant that additional work was needed to modify the pair intended for 'B' and 'X' locations.[235] More crucial was the fact that *Vanguard*'s magazines were below the shell rooms. This reversed the First World War practice around which the mountings had originally been built,[236] and meant adapting the below-decks structures and adding a powder-handling room.[237]

One point, not often stated in summary accounts,[238] is that *Vanguard* used only the 15-inch *mountings* from *Glorious* and *Courageous*, including the gun-houses and below-decks equipment.[239] The *guns* fitted to the mountings were drawn from a common pool comprising most of the 184 15-inch barrels that were manufactured, which were circulated around the fleet and rotated ashore as each needed relining.[240] In point of fact, the specific barrels used on *Vanguard* had previously been deployed on *Queen Elizabeth* (2), *Ramillies* (2), *Royal Sovereign* (1), *Resolution* (1), the monitor *Erebus* (1) and *Warspite* (1).[241] Work on *Vanguard*'s mountings was completed in 1944,[242] and the modified mountings were dubbed Mark I/N RP 12.[243]

Vanguard was launched on 30 November 1944,[244] two weeks after Germany's last battleship, *Tirpitz*, was sunk by the RAF.[245] Fitting out began with the aim of completing *Vanguard* by late 1945 for service with the British Pacific Fleet.[246] In late 1944 the Allies expected – and were planning for – a major ground campaign in Japan itself. Because of the priority given to the European war, such a campaign could not be initiated until early 1946. It was expected to take most of that year, perhaps into 1947, and to invoke up to a million casualties, including Japanese civilians.[247] As matters stood, war's end in August 1945 changed the calculation. *Vanguard* was too close to completion to abandon, but work slowed and she was not commissioned until April 1946.[248]

The Admiralty still hoped to resume the battleship programme post-war. Design work continued during 1944-45 on the *Lions*, by this stage substantially modified to include war experience. That included the fact that in late 1944, *Tirpitz* was sunk by means of 12,000-lb 'Tallboy' bombs.[249] Sketch plans prepared in January 1945 by the DNC of the day, Charles Lillicrap, indicated that a ship built to include the protection now thought necessary against air attack might displace up to 70,000 tons with a beam of 120 feet. Even then, Lillicrap felt, such a ship was going to be vulnerable. The cost of such a ship was also immense, and smaller editions with six 16-inch guns were then examined.[250]

By this time it was clear Britain's post-war navy was going to be a very different service from that of the 1930s, primarily for economic reasons. Britain had been in dire straits financially after the end of the First World War, a generation earlier. Now, in 1945, the situation was catastrophic. Britain had stood, alone for a time, against the darkness; but two decades of recession followed by six years of total war had effectively bankrupted the country. By 1945 two thirds of Britain's pre-war trade had been lost, and there seemed no chance of meeting massive balance-of-payments deficits. John Maynard Keynes warned the government in August 1945 that it was no longer going to be possible to maintain the Empire. Much of the war effort had been possible only via the US Lend Lease system, which was due to end, and he warned of a 'financial Dunkirk'.[251]

This calamity did not happen. The incoming Labour government was able to obtain loans from the United States and Canada – negotiated, in part, by Keynes.[252] That was joined by outright US support from 1947 via the Marshall Plan, ostensibly intended to rebuild a shattered Europe against the rise of the Soviet Union.[253] However, all this was simply a stop-gap, and in 1949 a balance-of-payments crisis prompted relatively massive devaluation of the pound.

There was no chance of maintaining significant military forces in the face of this ongoing financial crisis. Defence spending peaked at 52 percent of GDP in 1945,[254] but dramatic cut-backs began as war ended. Part of this view came from the fact that, although the Soviet Union was considered to be the next likely enemy, they were also regarded by the British Chiefs of Staff as unready for war. As late as 1947, the Chiefs of Staff did not think the Soviets could launch war on the west until 1956.[255] The Berlin crisis of

1948 and Korean War changed that perception, but British defence budgets nonetheless fell to under 6 percent of GDP by the end of the 1940s, rising again with the Korean War.[256]

The British Empire had, as Niall Ferguson put it, effectively gone into liquidation. This was the cost to Britain of defeating the Axis, and – as he pointed out – one that was known when Britain decided to stand, alone, in 1940.[257] Still, it took a while for the reality to sink in. The Suez Crisis of 1956, in which Britain and France attempted to maintain their influence over Egypt by military action – and failed – was the last gasp of the old mind-set. It could not be sustained.[258] Beneath all this was the hard fact that Britain was continuing to decline industrially; between 1950 and 1973, for example, Britain's share of world manufacturing exports dropped from 25 to 9 percent, and world share of merchant ship construction fell from 33 to 4 percent over the same period. [259]

The practical effect on the Royal Navy was dramatic. As the First Sea Lord, Admiral of the Fleet Sir Andrew Cunningham, recalled in his autobiography, the immediate aftermath of the Second World War was a busy time.[260] Ships under construction were cancelled 'on the stocks' or work slowed to a crawl. New naval programmes fell by the wayside, including plans to build four huge fleet carriers,[261] and this despite the focus on air power at sea.[262]

The pro-battleship lobby still had a voice; but although the Admiralty proposed the developed *Lion*-class battleships for the 1945 programme,[263] they were rejected in October.[264] Even then, there were suggestions that battleships remained essential to the fleet, and designs for 16-inch gun mountings were contemplated as late as March 1949.[265] Old traditions died hard, it seemed; and in context of the mood in some British government circles that the Empire could be maintained, such conservatism was perhaps not surprising. But in practise there was no chance of further battleships being built, even had the type not been eclipsed by technology.

This same constraint put paid to the careers of all older British battleships. At a time when the punch of the fleet came from aircraft carriers, and when the military role of battleships was swinging towards that of fleet escort and shore bombardment, Britain simply could not afford them. All but the four *King George V*'s and *Vanguard* were withdrawn from service soon after war's end, then sold for scrap in 1948-49.[266] Of the older ships only *Royal Sovereign*, which had been lent to Russia in 1944, served much longer; but that was only because she was not returned to Britain until 1949, at which point she too was sold for scrapping.[267]

Battleships still carried a certain prestige value – underscored when *Vanguard* was effectively converted into a royal yacht. She also served with NATO during the early 1950s, although there was a lack of gun-armed opponents, other than the Soviet *Sverdlov*-class cruisers.[268] War plans floated in 1951 gave the British battleship the task of destroying them, but whether *Vanguard* could have met the 90-day war readiness criteria was entirely another matter. By this time X-turret was non-operational, and *Vanguard* did not carry enough crew to operate all the magazines.[269] Such was the cost of cut-backs. Certainly the ship could not have adopted the traditional battleship role in case of more sudden outbreak of war. Indeed, by this time main armament ammunition was apparently not usually shipped.[270] The original design called for 100 rounds per gun,[271] a significant total weight,[272] and on first commission the battleship carried an additional 9 practise shells per gun.[273] But apart from standing concerns about structural strains on her hull, load had to be paid for operationally in terms of fuel. It was cheaper to run the ship light.

All this masked the fact that in many respects *Vanguard* was the pinnacle of British battleship design, the fastest and arguably all-round best battleship ever built for the Royal Navy. This was not surprising; her design drew from intensive work on the *King George V* and *Lion* classes and incorporated lessons from war experience. As we have seen, her main armament – as modified – was not far below early 1940s standards. Furthermore, *Vanguard*'s fire-control systems were the very latest available. Her underwater protection system was designed to resist a 1300lb TNT charge at optimal position, better than any previous British battleship.[274]

Vanguard was also fast, making some 31.57 knots on trial,[275] and she was an excellent sea-boat. According to one crew member, *Vanguard*'s 'gentle roll' in calmer waters provoked sea-sickness; but she could handle herself in heavy seas. During Exercise Mariner in 1953 she maintained higher speeds in gale conditions – reportedly 26 knots with a roll of 12 degrees,[276] than USS *Iowa*, although the American ship had higher maximum speed.[277] This was apparently a function of the fact that the US ship's hydrodynamics had been optimised for speed.[278] Observers aboard *Vanguard* described the 'spray flying out from either bow' of their ship as a 'magnificent sight'.[279]

More crucially, crew habitability standards were higher than previous heavy British ships, and included a 'superb laundry'.[280] She also had cafeteria-style dining, a shift from older-style messing aboard British battleships. This was a novelty and apparently not initially welcomed. But it became standard through Royal Navy.[281] And there was a cinema. All this made the ship a better home for the crew – a significant point, because the capability of a ship to do its intended job is defined as much by the ability of the crew as by lists of engineering statistics.

Vanguard, in short, was very much the last word in British battleship design – correcting prior issues and taking design thinking a step forward, and this in spite of the many pressures confronting her designers, ranging from industrial limits to war-driven shortages of material and labour. This was a remarkable achievement, although there were still points of criticism. Late in the war R. J. Daniel was sent to the Bath offices of the Department of Naval Construction to calculate the effects on *Vanguard* of torpedo hits and was dismayed to find that the 'message that we younger officers had tried to put over in 1942/43' in regard to asymmetric flooding had not been taken up.[282] As US naval architects William Garzke and R. O. Dulin observe, *Vanguard*'s propulsion plant employed more modest steam conditions than US systems.[283] While post-war tests indicated that British armour was superior to US Class 'A' armour, they argued that *Vanguard*'s overall armour scheme was not as good as might be expected on a ship of that size.[284] She did, however, have an excellent anti-aircraft battery for the day, in part because of the power-operated Bofors.[285]

All of it, of course, became academic. After a refit in 1955 *Vanguard* was taken out of service, becoming flagship of the Reserve Fleet in October 1956.[286] Here she provided sets for the film *Sink The Bismarck*.[287] By this time she was also Britain's last battleship; the *King George V* class were disposed of by 1957.[288] In October 1959 *Vanguard* too was put on the disposal list.[289] She was sold to the breakers for £560,000,[290] and – as we saw in the opening paragraphs - was towed out of Portsmouth for scrapping at Faslane in August 1960,[291] ending an era in British naval history.

The last years of that era had been characterised, as we have seen in this extended essay, by an increasing array of limiting factors. Financial, industrial, treaty and finally war constraints all worked together in complex ways to constrain British battleship design at every turn. Ultimately, those constraints ended Britain's battleship era; but – as we have seen – that did not reduce the effort by British naval designers to come up with the best answers to the challenges that this environment posed.

Notes

1. https://www.portsmouth.co.uk/lifestyle/heritage/what-really-happened-on-vanguard-that-fateful-day-in-portsmouth-harbour-1-6091906, accessed 26 October 2018.
2. See, e.g. Tony Gibbons, *The Complete Encyclopedia of Battleships and Battlecruisers*, Lansdowne Press, London 1983, p. 30.
3. Ibid, p. 80.
4. Ibid, pp. 170-71.
5. For background on the gold standard see, e.g. https://www.econlib.org/library/Enc/GoldStandard.html
6. https://www.ukpublicspending.co.uk/debt_brief.php
7. https://www.investopedia.com/terms/k/keynesianeconomics.asp
8. Speech to the House of Commons, 12 November 1936, https://speakola.com/political/winston-churchill-the-locust-years-1936
9. For details see, e.g. Ian Sturton (ed) *Conway's All The World's Battleships*, Conway Maritime Press, London 1987, pp. 124-128, 185-178.
10. See, e.g. ibid pp 68-76, compare with ibid pp. 175-178.
11. Christopher M. Bell, *Churchill and Sea Power*, Oxford University Press, Oxford 2013, p. 89.
12. Gibbons, pp. 228-229.
13. For that process see Norman Friedman, *The British Battleship 1906-46*, Seaforth, Barnsley, 2015, pp. 186-189.
14. D. K. Brown, *From Nelson to Vanguard: Warship design and development 1923-1945*, Seaforth, Barnsley, 2000, p. 19.
15. Friedman, *The British Battleship*, p. 209.
16. Ibid, p. 212.
17. Ibid, pp. 147-148.
18. Ibid, p. 210.
19. Ibid, p. 212.
20. Per inflation calculator at http://inflation.iamkate.com/
21. Noted in https://en.wikipedia.org/wiki/Type_45_destroyer

22	National Archives CAB/23/23, 'Cabinet 67(20), Conclusions of a meeting of the Cabinet, held at 10 Downing Street, S.W., on Wednesday, 8th December 1920, at 11.30 a.m.'.
23	Hunt, pp. 122-124.
24	Robert C. Stern, *The Battleship Holiday: the naval treaties and capital ship design*, Seaforth, Barnsley 2017, p. 94.
25	Ibid, p. 96.
26	See, e.g. Friedman, p. 213.
27	Stern, p. 97.
28	Robert C. Stern, *The Battleship Holiday: the naval treaties and capital ship design*, Seaforth, Barnsley 2017, p. 94.
29	Some accounts indicate the original four battlecruiser names, *Invincible, Inflexible, Indomitable* and *Indefatigable* were contemplated.
30	Friedman, *The British Battleship*, p. 212..
31	See, e.g. https://2001-2009.state.gov/r/pa/ho/time/id/88313.htm also https://www.globalsecurity.org/military/world/naval-arms-control-1921.htm, and: http://totallyhistory.com/washington-naval-conference/, also this http://www.u-s-history.com/pages/h1355.html and: http://www.digitalhistory.uh.edu/disp_textbook.cfm?smtID=3&psid=3995
32	Friedman, *The British Battleship*, p. 213.
33	Stern, p. 140.
34	See, e.g. https://history.state.gov/milestones/1921-1936/london-naval-conf
35	Various designs had been proposed as 'paper projects' during the interim. See William H. Garzke and Robert O. Dulin, *British, Soviet, French and Dutch battleships of World War II*, Jane's Publishing Company, London 1980, p. 168.For *Nelson* summary see Sturton (ed),pp. 92-93.
36	Ibid.
37	See, e.g. https://www.gracesguide.co.uk/Vickers
38	For discussion see Simon C. Holmes and Florian Poloeckl, 'Bank on Steel? Join Stock Banks and the Rationalisation of the British Interwar Steel Industry', *University of Oxford Discussion Papers on Economic and Social History*, No. 93, January 2012.
39	Ibid, p. 5.
40	For brief summary see https://en.wikipedia.org/wiki/Great_Depression_in_the_United_Kingdom
41	http://www.invergordon.info/TheMutiny
42	Chart in https://www.economicshelp.org/blog/5948/economics/uk-economy-in-the-1920s/
43	Garzke and Dulin, *British,Soviet, French and Dutch battleships of World War II*, pp. 168-169.
44	Figures in Brown, *Nelson to Vanguard*, p. 17, however Brown is incorrect relative to buying power vs price indices.
45	Garzke and Dulin, *British, Soviet, French and Dutch battleships of World War II*, pp. 226-227.
46	Naval Limitation Treaty (Second London Naval Treaty) of 25 March 1936, Part 2 Article 4 (2), text at https://www.loc.gov/law/help/us-treaties/bevans/m-ust000003-0257.pdf

47	Garzke and Dulin, *British, Soviet, French and Dutch battleships of World War II*, p. 202.
48	Winston Churchill, *The Second World War, III, The Grand Alliance*, Cassell & Co., London 1952, p. 781.
49	Garzke and Dulin, *British, Soviet, French and Dutch battleships of World War II*, p. 170
50	Ibid, p. 171.
51	Ibid, p. 173; Friedman, *The British Battleship*, p. 301.
52	Brown, *Nelson to Vanguard*, p. 20, 22.
53	Ibid, pp. 20-22.
54	Sturton (ed), p. 25.
55	Garzke and Dulin, *British, Soviet, French and Dutch battleships of World War II*, p. 172.
56	Sturton (ed), p. 178.
57	Robert O. Dulin and William H. Garzke, *Battleships: United States Battleships of World War II*, MacDonald and Janes, London, 1976, p. 34.
58	Garzke and Dulin, *British, Soviet, French and Dutch battleships of World War II*, p. 176.
59	Ibid.
60	Ibid, p. 231.
61	Winston Churchill, *The Second World War, I, The Gathering Storm*, Cassell & Co., London 1948, p. 127.
62	Garzke and Dulin, *British, Soviet, French and Dutch battleships of World War II*, p. 175.
63	Ibid.
64	Friedman, *The British Battleship 1906-46*, pp. 316-317.
65	Garzke and Dulin, *British, Soviet, French and Dutch battleships of World War II*, p. 240.
66	Ibid, p. 234.
67	Compare R. A. Burt, *British Battleships 1919-1945*, Seaforth, Barnsley 2012, p. 389, with Brown, *Nelson to Vanguard*, p. 34.
68	Noted in Brown, *Nelson to Vanguard*, p. 34.
69	Per inflation calculator at http://inflation.iamkate.com/, comparing 1936 with 2018.
70	Noted in https://en.wikipedia.org/wiki/Type_45_destroyer
71	Noted in https://en.wikipedia.org/wiki/HMS_Nelson_(28)
72	Calculated via http://inflation.iamkate.com/
73	Calculated via ibid.
74	Friedman, *The British Battleship 1906-46*, p. 336.
75	Ibid, p. 325.
76	Ian Raven and John Roberts, *British Battleships of World War Two: The Development and Technical History of the Royal Navy's Battleships and Battlecruisers from 1911 to 1946*, Arms & Armour Press, London 1976, p. 325.
77	Figures in Brown, *Nelson to Vanguard*, p. 18.
78	Naval Limitation Treaty (Second London Naval Treaty) of 25 March 1936, Part 2 Article 4 (2), text at https://www.loc.gov/law/help/us-treaties/bevans/m-ust000003-0257.pdf

79 See, e.g. Garzke and Dulin, *British, Soviet, French and Dutch battleships of World War II*, p. 173.
80 See https://www.navygeneralboard.com/the-king-george-v-class-better-battleships-than-history-usually-admits/ for discussion.
81 Naval Limitation Treaty (Second London Naval Treaty) of 25 March 1936, Part 2 Article 4 (2), text at https://www.loc.gov/law/help/us-treaties/bevans/m-ust000003-0257.pdf.
82 Discussed in Friedman, *The British Battleship 1906-46*, pp. 324-325.
83 Garzke and Dulin, *British, Soviet, French and Dutch battleships of World War II*, pp. 176-177.
84 Ibid, p. 176.
85 Noted in Friedman, *The British Battleship 1906-46*, p. 325.
86 Sturton (ed), pp. 25, 43.
87 Churchill, *The Second World War, I, The Gathering Storm*, p. 126.
88 Ibid, p. 126.
89 Ibid, p. 127.
90 Compare http://www.navweaps.com/Weapons/WNBR_14-45_mk7.php with http://www.navweaps.com/Weapons/WNBR_15-42_mk1.php
9 For list of known hits, see William H. Garzke and Robert O. Dulin, *Battleships: Axis and Neutral Battleships in World War II*, Jane's, London 1986, pp. 240-241. See also Brown, *Nelson to Vanguard*, p. 31.
92 Friedman, *The British Battleship 1906-46*, p. 319.
93 Compare statistics in, e.g. Sturton (ed), pp. 43,
94 Garzke and Dulin, *British, Soviet, French and Dutch battleships of World War II*, p. 215.
95 Brown, *Nelson to Vanguard*, p. 31.
96 http://www.navweaps.com/Weapons/WNBR_16-45_mk1.php
97 Noted in http://www.navweaps.com/Weapons/WNBR_14-45_mk7.php
98 Dulin and Garzke, *Battleships: United States Battleships of World War II*, p. 65.
99 Friedman, *The British Battleship 1906-46*, p. 313.
100 Dulin and Garzke, *Battleships: United States Battleships of World War II*, p. 56.
101 Ibid, *p. 52.*
102 Garzke and Dulin, *Battleships: British, Soviet, French and Dutch battleships of World War II*, p. 230.
103 Garzke and Dulin, *Battleships: British, Soviet, French and Dutch battleships of World War II*, pp. 180-190.
104 Dulin and Garzke, *Battleships: United States Battleships of World War II*, p. 46.
105 Garzke and Dulin, *Battleships: British, Soviet, French and Dutch battleships of World War II*, pp. 211-214.
106 Ibid, p. 219.
107 Including Dulin and Garzke, *Battleships: United States Battleships in World War II*, p. 107.
108 See Naval Limitation Treaty (Second London Naval Treaty) of 25 March 1936, Part 2 Article 4 (2), see text at https://www.loc.gov/law/help/us-treaties/bevans/m-ust000003-0257.pdf

109 Sturton (ed), pp. 26-27.
110 Ibid, pp. 107-108.
111 Ibid, pp. 44-45.
112 See, e.g. Dulin and Garzke, *United States battleships of World War II*, pp. 49-50.
113 Noted in Friedman, *The British Battleship 1906-36*, p. 329.
114 William H. McBride *Technological Change and the United States Navy*, 1865-1945, Johns Hopkins University Press, Baltimore, 2010 (paperback), p. 25.
115 Brown, *Nelson to Vanguard*, p. 12.
116 Ibid, p. 34.
117 Dulin and Garzke, *United States battleships of World War II*, p. 66; also Brown, *Nelson to Vanguard*, p. 34.
118 Dulin and Garzke, *United States battleships of World War II*, p. 66.
119 Sturton (ed), p. 44 cites *Bismarck* standard displacement at 41,700 tons, *Tirpitz* at 42,900.
120 Garzke and Dulin, *British, Soviet, French and Dutch battleships of World War II*, 170-171; Dulin and Garzke, *United States battleships of World War II*, pp. 70-71.
12   Garzke and Dulin, *British, Soviet, French and Dutch battleships of World War II*, pp. 170-171.
122 All tonnages are British 'long tons', per definition in the Naval Limitation Treaty (Second London Naval Treaty) of 25 March 1936, Article 1 (a) (3), https://www.loc.gov/law/help/us-treaties/bevans/m-ust000003-0257.pdf
123 Friedman, *The British Battleship 1906-46*, p. 327.
124 Ibid.
125 Ibid.
126 https://www.gracesguide.co.uk/George_Preece
127 Friedman, *The British Battleship 1906-46*, p. 327.
128 Garzke and Dulin, *British, Soviet, French and Dutch battleships of World War II*, p. 230.
129 Dulin and Garzke, *Battleships: United States Battleships in World War II*, pp 71-72.
130 Argued by Dulin and Garzke, *Battleships: United States Battleships in World War II*, pp 71, 95-96.
131 See, e.g. R. E. J Galilee, 'The Breakdown of Naval Limitation in the Far East – 1932-36', MA Thesis, University of Canterbury, 1975.
132 Dulin and Garzke, *Battleships: United States Battleships in World War II*, p. 110.
133 Ibid.
134 Ibid, pp 108-109. These were *not* the *Montana* class.
135 Naval Limitation Treaty (Second London Naval Treaty) of 25 March 1936, Part 2 Article 4 (2), text at https://www.loc.gov/law/help/us-treaties/bevans/m-ust000003-0257.pdf
136 Friedman, *The British Battleship 1906-36*, p. 329.
137 Beatty's flag-captain at Jutland.
138 See, e.g. Friedman, *The British Battleship 1906-36*, p. 329.
139 Ibid.
140 Ibid.

141	Dulin and Garzke, *Battleships: United States Battleships in World War II*, p. 113.
142	Friedman, *The British Battleship*, p. 329.
143	Brown, *Nelson to Vanguard*, p. 36.
144	See 'Limitation of Naval Armament: protocol signed at London, June 30 1938, modifying treaty of March 25, 1936', https://www.loc.gov/law/help/us-treaties/bevans/m-ust000003-0523.pdf
145	Dulin and Garzke, *Battleships: United States Battleships in World War II*, pp 112-115.
146	Friedman, *The British Battleship 1906-46*, p. 329.
147	July and June respectively, see Garzke and Dulin, *British, Soviet, French and Dutch battleships of World War II*, p. 263.
148	Design 30 kt (*Lion*) vs 28 (*King George V*), Ian Sturton (ed), pp. 93 and 98.
149	For details see http://www.navweaps.com/Weapons/WNBR_16-45_mk2.php
150	Brown, *Nelson to Vanguard*, p. 36.
151	Compare, e.g. the *Orion* (1909 programme), *King George V* (1910 programme) and *Iron Duke* (1911 programme) classes, see Sturton (ed), pp. 60-61, 66, 68-69.
152	The official Admiralty class name was *Revenge*, not *Royal Sovereign*, see Sturton (ed) p. 77.
153	See, e.g. ibid, pp. 60-78.
154	July and June respectively, see Garzke and Dulin, *British, Soviet, French and Dutch battleships of World War II*, p. 263.
155	Brown, *Nelson to Vanguard*, p. 36.
156	H. T. Lenton, *British and Empire Warships of the Second World War*, Naval Institute Press, 1998,
157	Ian Buxton and Ian Johnston, *The Battleship Builders: constructing and arming British capital ships*, Seaforth, Barnsley, 2013, p. 69.
158	Friedman, *The British Battleship 1906-46*, p. 325.
159	Raven and Roberts, p. 325.
160	The implication was that two ships used up six of the mountings, meaning a third ship could be laid down every third year using the seventh mounting built in the three consecutive prior years; but that was too slow for the war emergency, and other limitations included labour force availability and armour steel production, which by 1939 had already held up the *King George V* class.
161	Friedman, *The British Battleship 1906-46*, p. 336.
162	Ibid, p. 407, n. 25.
163	Two of the mountings were ordered in 1915 for HMS *Renown* and *Repulse* when originally ordered as 8-gun battleships, http://battleshiphmsvanguard.homestead.com/15inch.html
164	For brief discussion, see Sturton (ed), pp. 85-86.
165	http://battleshiphmsvanguard.homestead.com/cathro.html
166	Friedman, *The British Battleship 1906-46*, p. 336.
167	Ibid.
168	Ibid: Brown, *Nelson to Vanguard*, p. 37.
169	Friedman, *The British Battleship 1906-46*, p. 336.

170 B. Webster Smith HMS *Queen Elizabeth*, Blackie & Son, London 1940, pp. 148-177.
171 Norman Friedman, *Naval Weapons of World War I*, Seaforth, Barnsley 2011, pp. 43-46.
172 See, e.g. http://www.navweaps.com/Weapons/WNBR_15-42_mk1.php
173 Compare, e.g. tables in http://www.navweaps.com/Weapons/WNBR_15-42_mk1.php with tables for the US Mk VII 16-inch/50 http://www.navweaps.com/Weapons/WNUS_16-50_mk7.php
174 Materially higher velocities destabilised shells. See http://www.navweaps.com/Weapons/WNBR_15-42_mk1.php.
175 http://www.navweaps.com/Weapons/WNBR_14-45_mk7.php
176 See http://www.navweaps.com/Weapons/WNBR_15-42_mk1.php.
177 See, e.g. http://battleshiphmsvanguard.homestead.com/Specifications.html
178 Many were First World War vintage, see Sturton (ed) pp. 112-125.
179 Naval analyst D. K. Brown was of the opinion that *Vanguard* would have had a chance against *Yamato* as built. See Brown, *Nelson to Vanguard*, p. 38.
180 Friedman, *The British Battleship 1906-46*, p. 336.
181 Ibid.
182 Against the 16-inch guns of the *Nelson* class the immunity zone was calculated as between 16,500 to 33,250 yards. Garzke and Dulin, *British, Soviet, French and Dutch battleships of World War II*, p. 231.
183 Reproduced in Friedman, *The British Battleship 1906-46*, p. 337.
184 Ibid.
185 R. J. Daniel, *The End of an Era*, Periscope Publishing, Penzance, 2003, p. 10.
186 Sturton (ed), p. 98.
187 Friedman, *The British Battleship 1906-46*, p. 407, n.27.
188 Garzke and Dulin, *British, Soviet, French and Dutch battleships of World War II*, p. 224.
189 Sturton (ed), p. 98.
190 Ibid, p. 93.
191 https://www.winstonchurchill.org/resources/reference/churchills-political-offices-1906-1955/
192 http://www.naval-history.net/xGW-RNOrganisation1939-45.htm#12 – note that Phillips drowned when *Prince of Wales* was sunk in December 1941.
193 First Lord to Controller and others, 3 December 1939, in Winston Churchill, *The Second World War, I*, p. 592.
194 Ibid, p. 555.
195 Friedman, *The British Battleship 1906-46*, p. 338.
196 Ibid.
197 Ibid, p. 329.
198 Ibid, p. 338.
199 Roger Fry, 'HMS *Vanguard*: a short history of Britain's last battleship', *Vanguard*, No. 10 Area, October 2007, p. 16.
200 Raven and Roberts, p. 322.
201 https://www.winstonchurchill.org/resources/reference/churchills-political-offices-1906-1955/
202 Winston Churchill, *The Second World War, III*, p. 113.

203 Raven and Roberts, p. 322.
204 Winston Churchill, *The Second World War, III*, p. 781.
20 Ibid.
206 Brown, *Nelson to Vanguard*, p. 37.
207 Summarised in, e.g. Bernard Ireland, *The Illustrated Guide to Aircraft Carriers of the World*, Hermes House, London 2005, pp. 172-73.
20 Friedman, *The British Battleship 1906-46*, p. 335.
209 Ibid, p. 336.
210 For discussion see Garzke and Dulin, *British, Soviet, French and Dutch battleships of World War II*, p. 218-220.
211 See Matthew Wright, *Pacific War*, Reed, Auckland 2003, pp. 152-155.
212 Garzke and Dulin, *British, Soviet, French and Dutch battleships of World War II*, p. 224.
213 Only two were completed, after the war. Ireland, *The Illustrated Guide to Aircraft Carriers of the World*, p. 174-175.
214 For Cunningham's story in his own words see Viscount Cunningham of Hyndhope, *A Sailor's Odyssey*, Hutchison & Co, London 1951.
21 See, e.g. ibid, pp. 365-366.
216 Raven and Roberts, p. 322.
217 Matthew Wright, *Pacific War*, Reed, Auckland 2003, pp. 22-26.
218 Winston Churchill, *The Second World War, III*, p. 780.
219 Ibid. Tonnages are British 'long tons'.
220 Friedman, *The British Battleship 1906-46*, p. 339.
221 Ibid, p. 441.
22 Brown, *Nelson to Vanguard*, p. 38.
22 Friedman, *The British Battleship 1906-46*, p. 407 n. 30.
224 Ibid, p. 293.
225 Raven and Roberts, p. 325.
226 The issue included the interaction, during design, between displacement and freeboard, see Garzke and Dulin, *British, Soviet, French and Dutch battleships of World War II*, p. 175.
227 Friedman, *The British Battleship 1906-46*, p. 340.
228 R. J. Daniel, *The End of an Era*, p. 72.
229 Friedman, *The British Battleship 1906-46*, p. 340..
230 Brown, *Nelson to Vanguard*, p. 38.
231 http://battleshiphmsvanguard.homestead.com/15inch.html
232 Raven and Roberts, p. 339.
233 http://battleshiphmsvanguard.homestead.com/cathro.html
234 Raven and Roberts, p. 325.
235 http://www.navweaps.com/Weapons/WNBR_15-42_mk1.php#mountnote3
236 http://www.navweaps.com/Weapons/WNBR_15-42_mk1.php.
237 Ibid.
238 For example Antony Preston and John Bachelor, *Battleships 1919-77*, Phoebus, London, p. 58.
239 https://www.militaryfactory.com/ships/detail.asp?ship_id=HMS-Vanguard-23
240 http://www.navweaps.com/Weapons/WNBR_15-42_mk1.php, see also

	http://battleshiphmsvanguard.homestead.com/15inch.html
241	http://battleshiphmsvanguard.homestead.com/15inch.html
242	http://battleshiphmsvanguard.homestead.com/15inch.html
243	http://www.navweaps.com/Weapons/WNBR_15-42_mk1.php#mountnote3, but note that they were also labelled Mark I*/N RP 12
244	http://battleshiphmsvanguard.homestead.com/Specifications.html
245	Garzke and Dulin, *Axis and Neutral Battleships in World War II*, pp. 270-274.
246	For summary of BPF operations see, e.g. Matthew Wright, *Blue Water Kiwis*, Reed, Auckland 2000, pp. 139-144.
247	In 1945 the Allies expected to invade Japan; and Operation Coronet, the landing on Honshu, was planned for March 1946. The campaign was expected to last some months, see https://history.army.mil/books/wwii/MacArthur%20Reports/MacArthur%20V1/ch13.htm
248	See n.2 above.
249	Garzke and Dulin, *British, Soviet, French and Dutch battleships of World War II*, pp. 270-274.
250	Brown, *Nelson to Vanguard*, p. 39.
251	Cited in http://www.bbc.co.uk/history/british/modern/marshall_01.shtml
252	https://www.britannica.com/place/United-Kingdom/Britain-since-1945
253	Ibid.
254	https://www.ukpublicspending.co.uk/past_spending
255	Donald C. Watt, 'British Military Perceptions of the Soviet Union as a strategic threat' 1945-1950' in Josef Bekker and Franz Knipping (eds), *Great Britain, France, Italy and Germany in a Postwar World, 1945-1950*, Walter de Gruyter, Berlin, p. 332.
256	See, e.g. https://www.theguardian.com/news/datablog/2010/oct/18/historic-government-spending-area
257	Niall Ferguson *Empire: How Britain made the Modern World*, Penguin, London 2004, p. 362.
258	For discussion see, e.g. James Morris, *Farewell the Trumpets: An Imperial Retreat*, Penguin, London 1979, pp. 524-531; and Ferguson pp. 354-365.
259	Ferguson, p. 361.
260	Cunningham, p. 655.
261	The *Malta* class, see Ireland, *The Illustrated Guide to Aircraft Carriers of the World*, p. 176.
262	Cunningham, p. 655.
263	D. K. Brown *Rebuilding the Royal Navy:Warship design since 1945*, Seaforth, Barnsley, 2012, p. 19.
264	G. C. Peden, *Arms, Economics and British Strategy: from dreadnoughts to hydrogen bombs*, Cambridge University Press, Cambridge, 2007, p. 241.
265	Friedman, *The British Battleship 1906-46*, p. 367. Brown, N*elson to Vanguard*, p. 19, states 1948.
266	See, e.g. Sturton, pp. 71, 77, 84, 92.
267	Sturton, p. 78.
268	The world's last gun-armed cruisers, for brief summary see Bernard Ireland, *The Illustrated Guide to Cruisers*, Hermes House, London 2008, pp 238-239.

269	Peacetime complement was circa 1500 versus circa 2000 in wartime, see http://battleshiphmsvanguard.homestead.com/Specifications.html
270	Fry, p. 18.
271	Raven and Roberts, p. 339.
272	The various British 15-inch shells deployed during the Second World War (APC Mk XIIa, HE Mk VIIIb, etc) weighed 1935 lb each, see http://www.navweaps.com/Weapons/WNBR_15-42_mk1.php
273	http://www.navweaps.com/Weapons/WNBR_15-42_mk1.php
274	Sturton (ed) p. 99, noting that design specification and real-world performance often differed.
275	Compare speeds cited in ibid pp 50-98.
276	Fry, p. 19.
277	http://battleshiphmsvanguard.homestead.com/19534.html.
278	Many factors, including the relationship between ship length and average wave-peak distances, affect sea-keeping. For general discussion see http://www.worldnavalships.com/forums/archive/index.php/t-711-p-2.html
279	Quoted in Fry, p. 19.
280	http://www.worldnavalships.com/forums/archive/index.php/t-711-p-2.html
281	Brown, *Nelson to Vanguard*, p. 38.
282	R. J. Daniel, *End of an Era*, P. 72.
283	Garzke and Dulin, *British, Soviet, French and Dutch battleships of World War II*, p. 355.
284	Ibid.
285	Ibid, pp. 354-355.
286	Eric Grove, *The Royal Navy Since 1815: A New Short History*, Palgrave MacMillan, Basingstoke 2005.
287	http://www.imdb.com/title/tt0054310/
288	Garzke and Dulin, *British, Soviet, French and Dutch battleships of World War II*, p. 223.
289	https://www.facebook.com/pg/GreyFunnelLine/photos/?tab=album&album_id=634494469903023
290	Ibid.
291	http://battleshiphmsvanguard.homestead.com/DeathofaBattleship.html

Bibliography

Books and papers

Bell, Christopher M., *Churchill and Sea Power*, Oxford University Press, Oxford 2013.

Brown, D. K., *Rebuilding the Royal Navy: Warship design since 1945*, Seaforth, Barnsley, 2012.

Brown. D. K., *From Nelson to Vanguard: Warship design and development 1923-1945*, Seaforth, Barnsley, 2000.

Burt, R. A., *British Battleships 1919-1945*, Seaforth, Barnsley 2012.

Buxton, Ian and Ian Johnston, *The Battleship Builders: constructing and arming British capital ships*, Seaforth, Barnsley, 2013.

Churchill, Winston, *The Second World War, I, The Gathering Storm*, Cassell & Co., London 1948

Churchill, Winston, *The Second World War, III, The Grand Alliance*, Cassell & Co., London 1952.

Cunningham, Viscount Cunningham of Hyndhope (Andrew Browne), *A Sailor's Odyssey*, Hutchison & Co, London 1951.

Daniel, R. J., *The End of an Era*, Periscope Publishing, Penzance, 2003.

Ferguson, Niall, *Empire: How Britain made the Modern World*, Penguin, London 2004.

Friedman, Norman, *Naval Weapons of World War I*, Seaforth, Barnsley 2011.

Friedman, Norman, *The British Battleship 1906-46*, Seaforth, Barnsley, 2015.

Fry, Roger, 'HMS *Vanguard*: a short history of Britain's last battleship', *Vanguard*, No. 10 Area, October 2007.

Galilee, R. E. J., 'The Breakdown of Naval Limitation in the Far East – 1932-36', MA Thesis, University of Canterbury, 1975.

Garzke, William H., and Robert O. Dulin, *Battleships: Axis and Neutral Battleships in World War II*, Jane's, London 1986.

Garzke, William H., and Robert O. Dulin, *British, Soviet, French and Dutch battleships of World War II*, Jane's Publishing Company, London 1980.

Gibbons, Tony, *The Complete Encyclopedia of Battleships and Battlecruisers*, Lansdowne Press, London 1983.

Grove, Eric, *The Royal Navy Since 1815: A New Short History*, Palgrave MacMillan, Basingstoke 2005.

Holmes, Simon C. and Florian Poloeckl, 'Bank on Steel? Join Stock Banks and the Rationalisation of the British Interwar Steel Industry', University of Oxford Discussion Papers on Economic and Social History, No. 93, January 2012.

Ireland, Bernard, *The Illustrated Guide to Aircraft Carriers of the World*, Hermes House, London 2005/

Ireland, Bernard, *The Illustrated Guide to Cruisers*, Hermes House, London 2008.

Lenton, H. T., *British and Empire Warships of the Second World War*, Naval Institute Press, 1998.

McBride, William H., *Technological Change and the United States Navy, 1865-1945*, Johns Hopkins University Press, Baltimore, 2010.

Morris, James, *Farewell the Trumpets: An Imperial Retreat*, Penguin, London 1979.

Peden, G. C., *Arms, Economics and British Strategy: from dreadnoughts to hydrogen bombs*, Cambridge University Press, Cambridge, 2007.

Preston, Antony and John Bachelor, *Battleships 1919-77*, Phoebus, London.

Raven, Ian and John Roberts, *British Battleships of World War Two: The Development and Technical History of the Royal Navy's Battleships and Battlecruisers from 1911 to 1946*, Arms & Armour Press, London 1976.

Stern, Robert C., *The Battleship Holiday: the naval treaties and capital ship design*, Seaforth, Barnsley 2017.

Sturton, Ian (ed) *Conway's All The World's Battleships*, Conway Maritime Press, London 1987.

Watt, Donald C., 'British Military Perceptions of the Soviet Union as a

strategic threat' 1945-1950' in Josef Bekker and Franz Knipping (eds), *Great Britain, France, Italy and Germany in a Postwar World, 1945-1950*, Walter de Gruyter, Berlin.
Webster Smith, B., *HMS Queen Elizabeth*, Blackie & Son, London 1940.
Wright, Matthew, *Blue Water Kiwis*, Reed, Auckland 2000.
Wright, Matthew, *Pacific War*, Reed, Auckland 2003.

Websites

2001-2009.state.gov/r/pa/ho/time/id/88313.htm
battleshiphmsvanguard.homestead.com
en.wikipedia.org
gracesguide.co.uk
history.army.mil/
history.state.gov
inflation.iamkate.com/
speakola.com/
totallyhistory.com
www.bbc.co.uk/
www.britannica.com
www.digitalhistory.uh.edu
www.econlib.org
www.economicshelp.org/
www.globalsecurity.org
www.invergordon.info
www.investopedia.com
www.loc.gov/law/help/us-treaties/bevans/m-ust000003-0257.pdf
www.navweaps.com/
www.navygeneralboard.com
www.portsmouth.co.uk
www.theguardian.com
www.ukpublicspending.co.uk
www.ukpublicspending.co.uk/
www.u-s-history.com
www.winstonchurchill.org

About the author

Matthew Wright is a New Zealand writer with over thirty years professional experience as a published author and in publishing. He has qualifications in writing, music and anthropology among other fields, and holds multiple post-graduate degrees in history. He is a Fellow of the Royal Historical Society at University College, London.

Matthew Wright's New Zealand Military Series

Collect the set

www.ingramcontent.com/pod-product-compliance
Lightning Source LLC
Chambersburg PA
CBHW050706160426
43194CB00010B/2027